# THE CELTICS

## IN BLACK AND WHITE

Perhaps the most important moment in Celtics history occurred when owner Walter Brown hired Red Auerbach in 1950. In six decades in Boston, Auerbach has made history as head coach, general manager, and president of the Celtics. Auerbach said it best when he commented, "The Celtics aren't just a team, they're a way of life." (Courtesy of the Boston Herald.)

*On the front cover*: Pictured are the 1957-58 Boston Celtics. (Courtesy of the Sports Museum.)

*On the back cover*: Please see page 90. (Photograph by Tom Miller, courtesy of the photographer.)

# THE CELTICS
## IN BLACK AND WHITE

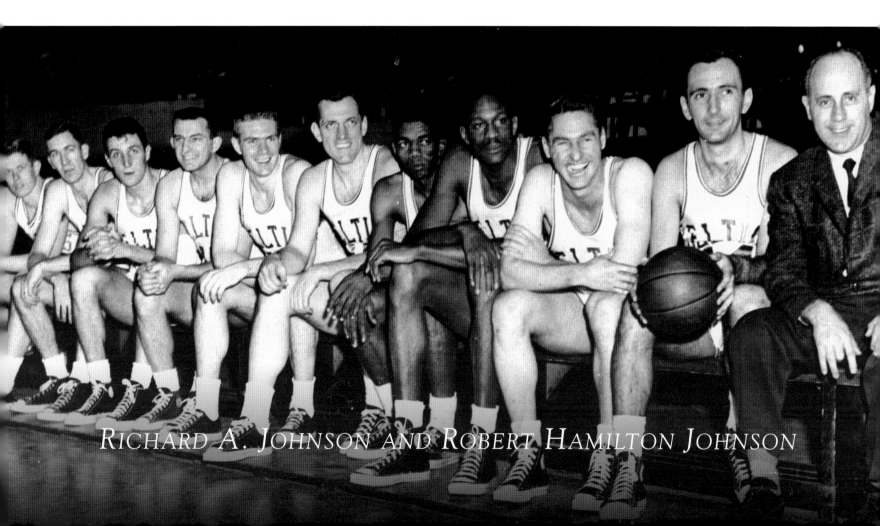

Richard A. Johnson and Robert Hamilton Johnson

Published by Arcadia Publishing
Charleston, South Carolina

Printed in the United States of America

Library of Congress Catalog Card Number: 2006923704

For all general information contact Arcadia Publishing at:
Telephone 843-853-2070
Fax 843-853-0044
E-mail sales@arcadiapublishing.com
For customer service and orders:
Toll-Free 1-888-313-2665

Visit us on the Internet at www.arcadiapublishing.com

*For our hero, Mary Hamilton Johnson.*

*In honor of every player privileged to wear Celtics green and in memory of the following members of the Celtics family: Walter Brown, an incomparable sportsman and the founder of the Celtics; Chuck Cooper, basketball pioneer; Howie McHugh, Walter Brown's right-hand man and a genuine Boston character; Walter Randall, equipment manager and gentleman; Johnny Most, the passionate voice of the Celtics; Reggie Lewis, possessor of an incomparable smile, gentle nature, and great game, who left us too soon.*

# CONTENTS

# FOREWORD

When I arrived in Boston in the late summer of 1970 to prepare for my first Celtics training camp, I was aware that I was joining a very special organization. It was my privilege to join a team that had captured 11 NBA championships, many of which were won by the players with whom I'd scrimmage as I sought to make my mark in the NBA. Veterans such as John Havlicek, Satch Sanders, and Don Nelson soon became friends and mentors as I absorbed the finer points of the Celtics tradition.

Not only are the Celtics one of the only two NBA charter franchises (along with the Knicks) to play in their city of origin, but more importantly they possess the greatest championship tradition in NBA history. This incredible story is captured by my friend and Sports Museum colleague Richard Johnson and his son Rob in this comprehensive illustrated history. This book was a labor of love for them, both as fans of the Celtics and because they have donated 100 percent of the royalties of this book to the museum.

Please enjoy this story and also visit the museum, which is located within the TD BankNorth Garden just below the rafters that contain 16 Celtics championship banners and the retired numbers of the players whose heroics you will discover in these pages.

—Dave Cowens, Trustee, the Sports Museum
Member, Basketball Hall of Fame

# INTRODUCTION

For six decades the Celtics have represented the best and worst of Boston, often at the same time. In the sunshine of their first dynasty of the late 1950s through the mid-1960s, the Celtics were nothing less than America's most successful and conspicuous example of Dr. Martin Luther King's dream of a society where blacks and whites could strive together toward a common goal while working in harmony. The feats of Bill Russell, Bob Cousy, Tom Heinsohn, K. C. Jones, Sam Jones, Jim Loscutoff, and company were reminiscent in their own way to the achievement and example set a generation earlier by a band of similarly courageous and multiracial performers named Benny Goodman, Teddy Wilson, Harry James, and Lionel Hampton, who achieved immortality at the famous Carnegie Hall Jazz Concert of 1938.

Both sets of performers entertained a large and diverse audience as they redefined their craft while setting an example that inspires to this day. For the fledgling NBA, Boston became the proverbial "City on a Hill," and for the past 60 years, the Boston Celtics have been nothing less than the most successful franchise in North American professional sports, as well its greatest exemplars of the American Dream.

At first, however, despite being granted this amazing team, Bostonians reacted with shocking indifference to a team that won 9 of 10 NBA titles starting in 1957. This included an unprecedented and never to be duplicated eight straight from 1959 to 1966. Crowds at most games at the Boston Garden were below 10,000, and the team was forced to resort to ambitious promotional schemes, which included staging doubleheaders with other NBA foes, the Harlem Globetrotters, the Harlem Magicians, and even Somerville High School in its Tech Tournament salad days in the early 1950s.

As a kid growing up in Worcester in the 1960s, I thought the original address of my favorite team was perfect, Boston Celtics, Boston Garden, Boston, 14, Massachusetts. I was convinced the post office was secretly honoring Bob Cousy, the man who virtually invented the position of point guard and whose behind-the-back passes became a feat to be imitated nearly as much as that New England male rite of passage known as a badly performed Johnny Most impression.

# ACKNOWLEDGMENTS

For the past quarter century, I have worked as curator of the Sports Museum, located within the TD BankNorth Garden and just yards away from the Celtics parquet. It is my privilege to serve as steward of the greatest regional sports heritage on the planet. As part of my job, I am often asked by visitors from across the globe to show them our Celtics treasures, such as the team's first 24-second clock and our treasure trove of team uniforms, trophies, photographs, and video highlights.

For decades, the Celtics connection to the Sports Museum has remained strong as former players Dave Cowens and Mal Graham have led the museum board of trustees, as has former Celtics general manager Jan Volk. This book, written with my son, Robert, is both our gift to the museum and our homage to the incredible heritage of the Celtics on the occasion of their 60th anniversary. All royalties from this book are being donated to the Sports Museum, a nonprofit educational organization.

We would like to thank the following people for their help in creating this book: the *Boston Herald* library staff of John Cronin and Al Thibeault were instrumental in making this book possible, as were Rich Gotham, Jeff Twiss, and Keith Sliney of the Boston Celtics; Brian and Steve Babineau of Sports Action Images; Steve Lipofsky; Greg Lee of the *Boston Globe*; George Sullivan, whose *Picture History of the Boston Celtics* is indispensable; Dave Cowens; the Sports Museum staff of Rusty Sullivan (whose initial edit of the text was invaluable and above and beyond the call of duty), Brian Codagnone, Michele Gormley, and the late Gordon Katz; photographer Pamela Schuyler-Cowens; Michele Lee Amundsen; Tiffany Howe of Arcadia Publishing; and our own home team of Boston Celtics named Minna Flynn Johnson, Mary Hamilton Johnson, Lizzy, and Toby Philip Jenkins.

Red Auerbach enjoys a cigar in the comfort of his office. (Courtesy of the Boston Celtics.)

# THE 1940S AND 1950S

Walter Brown founded the Celtics in 1946, and his team remains one of two NBA teams, along with the New York Knickerbockers, that have remained in their original cities since the founding of the league. Brown, shown here in his Boston Garden office, was both passionate and versatile. Not only did he start Hockey USA, but he also ran both the Boston Bruins and Boston Olympics hockey teams. He also started the Ice Capades and ran the Boston Garden for two generations. (Courtesy of the Sports Museum.)

The 1946–1947 Celtics divided their time between the Boston Arena and the Boston Garden while posting a mediocre 22-38 sixth-place finish. Pictured from left to right are the following: (first row) Dutch Garfinkle, Charlie Hoefer, Honey Russell, John Simmons, and Wyndol Gray; (second row) Harvey Cohn, Al Brightman, Art Spector, Harold Kottman, Connie Simmons, Gerard Kelly, and Danny Silva. (Courtesy of the Boston Celtics.)

Chuck Connors, pictured here as Lucas McCain in *The Rifleman*, also starred in *Branded* and was featured in countless other acting roles, including a stint in the Boston-based series *Spenser: for Hire*. In his episode on the 1980s show, he played a gangster who, at one point in the program, is filmed attending a Celtics game at the Boston Garden. (Courtesy of the Sports Museum.)

Connie Simmons was half of the first and only brother combination in Celtics history, along with his older brother John. In the Celtics' inaugural season, Connie led the Celtics in points per game (with 10.3), field-goal percentage (.320), free-throw percentage (.667), and assists (62 in 60 games). (Courtesy of the Boston Herald.)

"Big Ed" Sadowski was the Celtics' first genuine star. Named All-League for the 1947–1948 season, the six-foot-five-inch center finished third in league scoring with 19.4 points per game while leading Boston to its first ever playoff appearance against the Chicago Stags. (Courtesy of the Boston Herald.)

Another of the interesting characters in early team history was guard Saul Mariaschin. The Harvard graduate was also a published songwriter and the Celtics' third-round draft pick in 1947. In his one season in Boston, Mariaschin finished third among Celtics scorers (7.7 points per game) and was in the top 10 in league assists. (Courtesy of the Boston Herald.)

Former Dartmouth and Holy Cross coach Alvin "Doggie" Julian replaced Honey Russell on April 11, 1948, in a move that Walter Brown hoped would help attract a large portion of the sellout crowds that Julian's Holy Cross squads brought to Boston Garden. In two seasons in Boston, Julian's Celtics finished with a dismal combined record of 47-81 as the team nearly folded. (Courtesy of the Sports Museum.)

In their search for box office attractions, the Celtics tapped Holy Cross for many players, including the duo of George Kaftan (left) and Dermie O'Connell. The two had helped lead Holy Cross to the 1947 NCAA title and had filled the Boston Garden for the countless games the Crusaders had trekked to Boston for lucrative "home" games against national competition. (Courtesy of the Boston Herald.)

Guard Joe Mullaney was another of the former Holy Cross stars who made his way to Boston. In limited service with the Celtics, Mullaney averaged only 0.8 points per game. He later achieved great fame as a coach while leading the Providence College Friars, Los Angeles Lakers, and seven other professional and college teams. (Courtesy of the Boston Herald.)

ECCENTRIC
DANCING

An Evening with
Tony Lavelli

GROTESQUE
PANTOMINE

MUSICAL
SATIRE

COMEDY
MONOLOGS

SCENES FROM

ACT 2

"Songs,

Dance &

Comedy!"

From left to right, former Dartmouth star Ed Leede, Yale and Somerville High School standout Tony Lavelli, and George Kaftan pose at practice in 1949. Not only was Lavelli the team's first draft pick in 1949, but he also entertained crowds with performances on his accordion at halftime. The NBA paid the former consensus All-American $125 for 25 halftime performances. Alas, despite several brilliant games in which he scored 26 points against the champion Lakers and 28 points (twice) against the Knicks, the Celts finished in last place. (Courtesy of the Sports Museum.)

Following his brief NBA career, Tony Lavelli took his act on the road as a versatile entertainer. (Courtesy of the Boston Herald.)

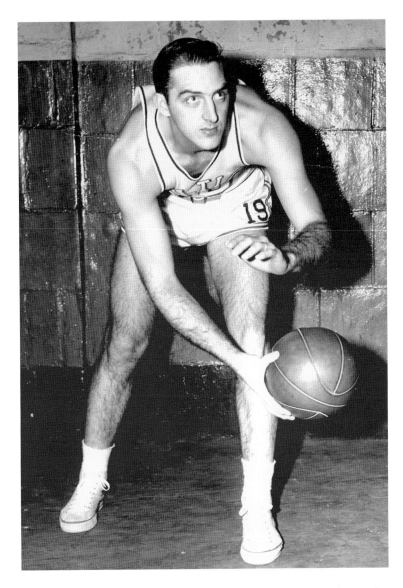

Center John Manhken served as the backup to all-star center Ed Macauley for the 1951–1952 and 1952–1953 seasons. The former Georgetown star was one of the first of coach Arnold "Red" Auerbach's role players. His role as the rugged enforcer would later be embraced by the likes of Bob Brannum, Jim Loscutoff, and Greg Kite, among others on future Celtics teams. (Courtesy of the Boston Herald.)

Ed Leede was one of the last of a string of local collegiate stars brought to Boston in the hope of attracting fans based on their undergraduate heroics. In two seasons with the Celtics, the former Dartmouth star scored a respectable 7.8 points per game. (Courtesy of the Boston Herald.)

Brooklyn-born Red Auerbach was brought to the Celtics by Walter Brown in 1950 with the formidable task of saving the franchise. Prior to Auerbach's arrival, the team was losing over $100,000 a year and was in danger of folding. Auerbach was asked to both bolster attendance and make the playoffs. The 32-year-old mentor succeeded on both fronts and soon made the franchise one of America's sports treasures.

Former Washington Capitals John Manhken (left) and Sonny Hertzberg were reunited with the Celtics in 1949 and were soon joined by former Capitals coach Red Auerbach. The pair is shown prior to a Boston Garden doubleheader that saw the Celtics play the Anderson (Indiana) Packers following a game between the Chicago Stags and Baltimore Bullets. (Courtesy of the Boston Herald.)

Walter Brown made NBA history in the 1950 draft when he chose Chuck Cooper of Duquesne with the team's second-round pick. This selection marked the first time an African American had been drafted by an NBA team. When asked about his choice by a fellow owner concerned with the implications of the choice, Brown remarked, "I don't give a damn if he's striped, polka dot, or plaid. Boston takes Charles Cooper of Duquesne." (Courtesy of the Boston Celtics.)

Among the legion of future coaches to play for the Celtics was Horace "Bones" McKinney. The former North Carolina State star was player-coach for the Washington Capitals in their last season of 1950–1951. He arrived in Boston in time for the 1951 playoffs and played the following season for the Celtics as a forward. McKinney later coached the Carolina Cougars of the American Basketball Association. (Courtesy of the Boston Herald.)

Bob Harris (left) and Bob Brannum were both known as tough customers in the old-school NBA, where rough play was celebrated. These early Celtics role players are depicted as they suited up prior to the Celtics' playoff opener against the New York Knicks on March 20, 1951. Boston lost the best of three series by two games to nil. (Courtesy of the Boston Herald.)

All-star guard Bill Sharman, shown here with Boston sportswriting legend Dave "the Colonel" Egan, arrived in Boston from the Fort Wayne Pistons in one of the most one-sided trades in basketball history. The Celtics acquired Sharman and Bob Brannum in exchange for the draft rights to Bowling Green center Chuck Share in 1951. Sharman would enjoy a hall of fame career with the Celtics while playing on four world championship teams. He later coached the Los Angeles Lakers to the 1972 title. (Courtesy of the Boston Herald.)

From left to right, Celtics center Ed Macauley, owner Walter Brown, and Kenny Sailors are shown at the opening of preseason training camp at the Naval Recreational Building on Boston's waterfront. Both players came to Boston via the NBA dispersal draft after Macauley's St. Louis Bombers and Sailors's Denver Nuggets ceased operations. Macauley soon became an all-star, and Sailors played only a handful of games for the Celtics before joining the Baltimore Bullets. (Courtesy of the Boston Herald.)

From left to right, Sonny Hertzberg, Ed Macauley, and Kenny Sailors are shown at Celtics training camp in November 1950. Each player had led his respective team in scoring the previous season, with Hertzberg scoring 697 points for the Celtics, Macauley scoring 1,081 for the St. Louis Bombers, and Sailors scoring 989 for the Denver Nuggets. All three were members of Red Auerbach's first Celtics squad. (Photograph by Joe Parodi, courtesy of the Boston Herald.)

Pictured here is the program for the first ever NBA All-Star Game at the Boston Garden on March 2, 1951. Prior to the game, Celtics owner Walter Brown prayed for a crowd of 10,000 in order for the NBA's first ever All-Star Game to break even. Nearly 100 extra fans made his wish come true as the less-than-capacity crowd saw the East All-Stars led by hometown favorite Ed Macauley beat the West All-Stars by a score of 111-94. (Courtesy of the Sports Museum.)

The luck of the Irish was surely with the Celtics on October 5, 1950, when the team obtained the services of Bob Cousy. The Celtics drew Cousy's name from a hat when the Chicago Stags (to whom Cousy had been traded by the Tri-City Blackhawks) folded and their players became available to the Celtics. The $8,500 fee paid by Boston to the league for Cousy's services may have been the greatest investment in franchise history. (Courtesy of the Walter Brown Collection, the Sports Museum.)

Celtics strongman Bob Brannum is shown with his daughter at Celtics practice. Following a two-year stint with the Sheboygan Redskins, Brannum arrived in Boston in the autumn of 1951. He soon became Red Auerbach's enforcer, a solid but bruising presence for the rapidly improving Celtics. Brannum later served as head coach at Brandeis University. (Courtesy of the Sports Museum.)

Dr. Jack E. Nichols (right) is shown receiving the alumni association award for dental surgery from Tufts University School of Dental Medicine dean Cyril D. Marshall. Following his five-year Celtics career, which included his membership on the first world championship team of 1957, Nichols returned home to Seattle where he served as a dentist for many years. (Courtesy of the Sports Museum.)

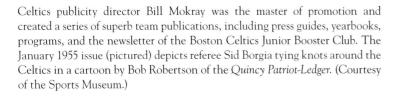

Celtics publicity director Bill Mokray was the master of promotion and created a series of superb team publications, including press guides, yearbooks, programs, and the newsletter of the Boston Celtics Junior Booster Club. The January 1955 issue (pictured) depicts referee Sid Borgia tying knots around the Celtics in a cartoon by Bob Robertson of the *Quincy Patriot-Ledger*. (Courtesy of the Sports Museum.)

Bob Cousy surges past Ernie Vanderweghe of the Knicks in fourth-quarter action in the first playoff game of the 1953 Eastern Division Finals at Madison Square Garden. Watching Cousy are Knicks Dick McGuire (No. 15), Carl Braun (No. 4) and Nat "Sweetwater" Clifton. The Celtics lost by a score of 95-91 despite Cousy's 28 points. (Courtesy of the Sports Museum.)

Celtics founder and owner Walter Brown (left) congratulates Bob Cousy (seated) on his legendary 50-point game against Syracuse in the 1953 playoffs in the Celtics locker room at the Boston Garden. In the marathon game, Cousy converted 30 of 32 free throws and scored 25 of his points in four overtimes to help lead Boston to victory in a game that put the then titleless franchise on the national basketball map. (Courtesy of the Sports Museum.)

In 1953, the Celtics made Kentucky star Frank Ramsey their first-round draft choice. Nicknamed the "Kentucky Colonel," Ramsey became the first "sixth man" in NBA history as Red Auerbach created a new basketball strategy with his effective use of the versatile Ramsey. (Courtesy of the Sports Museum.)

Celtics all-star guard Bill Sharman was given a "day" by the team on March 13, 1955, as Boston fans cheered he and his wife at the Boston Garden prior to the Celtics-Knicks game. Sharman arrived in Boston shortly after having worn the uniform of the Brooklyn Dodgers as a late-season call-up by the pennant contenders. He made history as the only major-leaguer to be thrown out of a game despite never seeing service (he was ejected from the dugout after shouting at an umpire). His luck in basketball was better as he formed a dream backcourt with Bob Cousy for the 1950s Celtics. (Photograph by Myer Ostroff, Boston Record.)

Known to fans simply as "Jungle Jim," Jim Loscutoff arrived in Boston from the University of Oregon as the Celtics first-round draft pick in 1955. The six-foot-five-inch forward soon made a name by replacing Bob Brannum as the Celtics enforcer and all-around tough guy. In a little over eight full seasons in Boston, Loscutoff played for five world champions. He later gained a share of immortality by being named the only player in franchise history to have his nickname, "Loscy," retired by the team. His No. 18 had already been retired in honor of Dave Cowens. (Courtesy of the Boston Herald.)

Jim Loscutoff (left) shows some of the fire that led to his ejection from 40 games during his Celtics career. Loscy was beloved by fans and teammates alike for his toughness and take-no-prisoners style of play. (Courtesy of the Sports Museum.)

Bob Cousy (right) and Frank Ramsey (center) greet the Celtics 1954 first-round draft choice, Togo Palazzi of Holy Cross. At Holy Cross, Palazzi helped lead the Crusaders to the 1954 National Invitation Tournament title, a tournament that at the time was viewed as the equal of the NCAA championship. Palazzi lasted a little over two seasons in Boston before joining the Syracuse Nats for the latter part of the 1956–1957 season. (Courtesy of the Sports Museum.)

Bill Russell battles against the St. Louis Hawks at Boston Garden in 1957. The two teams soon met in an epic NBA championship final that saw Boston capture its first world title with a 125-123 double-overtime victory in game seven at Boston Garden. Typical of Celtics games at that time, tickets were available until an hour prior to game time. (Courtesy of the Sports Museum.)

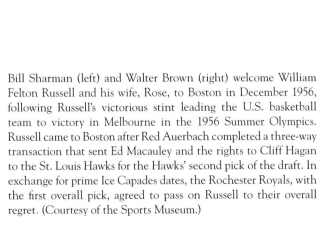

Bill Sharman (left) and Walter Brown (right) welcome William Felton Russell and his wife, Rose, to Boston in December 1956, following Russell's victorious stint leading the U.S. basketball team to victory in Melbourne in the 1956 Summer Olympics. Russell came to Boston after Red Auerbach completed a three-way transaction that sent Ed Macauley and the rights to Cliff Hagan to the St. Louis Hawks for the Hawks' second pick of the draft. In exchange for prime Ice Capades dates, the Rochester Royals, with the first overall pick, agreed to pass on Russell to their overall regret. (Courtesy of the Sports Museum.)

NBA Rookie of the Year Tommy Heinsohn played the game of his life in the seventh game of the 1957 NBA Finals at Boston Garden on April 13, 1957, leading the Celtics in scoring with 37 points in a game that went to two overtimes versus the St. Louis Hawks. After Heinsohn fouled out, he thought he may have cost the Celtics the title, only to be hoisted on the shoulders of jubilant fans minutes later. (Courtesy of the Sports Museum.)

# THE 1960S

The Celtics of the 1960s dominated professional basketball like no other team in any sport. The 1963 team celebrates its fifth consecutive world championship at Boston Garden. Pictured from left to right are the following: (first row) Bob Cousy, Frank Ramsey, and John Havlicek; (second row) Bill Russell, K. C. Jones, Tom "Satch" Sanders, Red Auerbach, and Tom Heinsohn. (Courtesy of the Boston Globe.)

Basketball's greatest champion was not the game's greatest scorer; however, Bill Russell worked tirelessly on his shooting and retired with an impressive point total of 14,522 to go with his franchise-leading 21,620 rebounds. (Courtesy of the Boston Herald.)

Bob Cousy was a master of what the late Al McGuire used to call "French pastry," the fancy no-look pass. He developed his skills on the playgrounds of Queens and dazzled crowds at Holy Cross, where his showmanship led writers to dub the team as the then "Fancy Pants AC." Here Cousy is seen in playoff action against the Cincinnati Royals at the Boston Garden. (Courtesy of the Sports Museum.)

Guard K. C. Jones was one of the trio of hall of famers chosen by the Celtics in the 1956 NBA draft along with University of San Francisco teammate Bill Russell and Holy Cross forward Tom Heinsohn. Jones is one of the greatest winners in American sports history, having joined the Celtics following back-to-back NCAA titles and an Olympic gold medal–winning performance. In nine seasons as a player in Boston, he won eight world championships. He won another two in his five seasons as head coach of the Celtics. (Courtesy of the Boston Globe.)

The world champion Celtics used the eighth pick of the 1957 draft to select little-known Sam Jones of North Carolina Central. In 12 seasons with the Celtics, Jones more than made a name for himself as a member of 10 world championship teams. (Courtesy of the Sports Museum.)

Red Auerbach used the perfect blend of street smarts and book learning to get the most out of his team. The tough Brooklyn kid learned the game both at Eastern District High School and at George Washington University, where he earned both his bachelor's and master's degrees (education). His book *Basketball for the Player, the Fan and the Coach* has been translated into many languages and is considered the finest book on the game. (Courtesy of the Boston Herald.)

In 1960, the Celtics used the eighth pick of the first round of the NBA draft to select forward Tom "Satch" Sanders of New York University. Sanders developed into one of the best defensive players in NBA history while helping lead the Celtics to eight world championships in 13 seasons. While sacrificing personal statistics, Sanders accepted his nightly assignment of covering—and shutting down—the likes of Elgin Baylor, Bob Pettit, and Dolph Schayes, among others. (Courtesy of the Boston Celtics.)

In the 1960s, Bill Russell spoke out on many social issues and was one of the most prominent, thoughtful, and outspoken leaders in America. Not only did he and Cleveland Browns star Jim Brown stand in support of Muhammad Ali in his antiwar stance, but Russell also took time to march for civil rights and speak to countless community groups about social justice. (Courtesy of the Sports Museum.)

Coach Red Auerbach got a lesson in rapid firing of a rifle by the rifleman himself, Chuck Connors, when the Celtics visited Connors, a former Celtic himself, on the Hollywood lot where he made his television series. Celtics in the background include Frank Ramsey, trainer Buddy LeRoux, Tommy Heinsohn, Bob Cousy, Sam Jones, K. C. Jones, Bill Russell, Gene Guarilia, and Bill Sharman. (Courtesy of the Sports Museum.)

Community service has been a staple of the Celtics organization for generations. Here Ruth Savel (left) and Esther Natole of Brookline tie a banner in support of Aid to Crippled Children on Dan Swartz (second from the left) and Jim Loscutoff of the Celtics. The Celtics helped the women in their collection to aid the cause sponsored by the United Order of True Sister Naomi No. 11 Boston Chapter. (Courtesy of the Boston Herald.)

Red Auerbach battled as hard as any of his players while ranting nightly at referees. Not only did he serve the team as coach and general manager, but he also assisted on a dozen other duties, which he remarked were later covered by at least that many executives in the team's organizational flowchart. Seated to the left of Auerbach is team trainer Edward "Buddy" Leroux, whose "Horatio Alger–esque" rise saw him become an eventual part owner of both the Red Sox and Suffolk Downs. (Courtesy of the Sports Museum.)

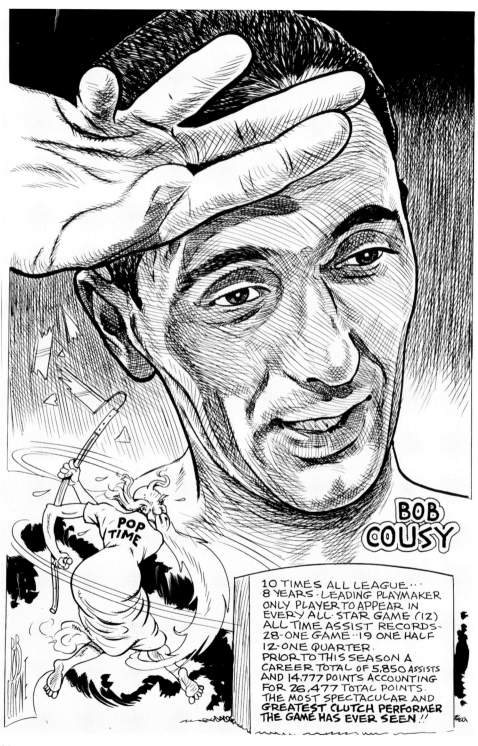

BOB COUSY

10 TIMES ALL LEAGUE···
8 YEARS·LEADING PLAYMAKER
ONLY PLAYER TO APPEAR IN
EVERY ALL·STAR GAME (12)
ALL TIME ASSIST RECORDS-
28·ONE GAME···19 ONE HALF
12·ONE QUARTER.
PRIOR TO THIS SEASON A
CAREER TOTAL OF 5,850 ASSISTS
AND 14,777 POINTS ACCOUNTING
FOR 26,477 TOTAL POINTS.
THE MOST SPECTACULAR AND
GREATEST CLUTCH PERFORMER
THE GAME HAS EVER SEEN !!

Holy Cross record breaker Jack "the Shot" Foley (right) is presented a game ball by fellow Crusaders Bob Cousy (left) and Tom Heinsohn during brief ceremonies immediately after the college star had set a new Crusader career–scoring record. Within the year, the Celtics made Foley the 16th overall pick of 1962. Foley saw limited action for the 1962–1963 world champions and later played for the Knicks. (Courtesy of the Sports Museum.)

In his 13 seasons, Bob Cousy was nothing less than the heart and soul of a Celtics team that grew from also-rans to the greatest dynasty in basketball history. (Cartoon by Bob Coyne.)

Surrounded by his family and teammates on his day, Bob Cousy broke down several times while thanking Boston, the Celtics, and the NBA for helping make his career a fulfilling and glorious experience. (Courtesy of the Boston Herald.)

# BOB COUSY DAY
## BOSTON CELTICS
### NATIONAL BASKETBALL ASSOCIATION

BOB COUSY

TEX

**BOSTON GARDEN, MARCH 17, 1963**

SOUVENIR PROGRAM *50¢*

The program was printed for Bob Cousy Day on March 17, 1963. Cousy's retirement was celebrated more than a month before his final game in a pregame ceremony that lasted nearly an hour and proved to be one of the most emotional events in Boston sports history. (Courtesy of Richard A. Johnson.)

On St. Patrick's Day in 1963, many Boston fans wept openly as they paid tribute to the Celtics' first superstar and the player who virtually invented the position of point guard. During an emotional pregame ceremony, when Cousy became overcome with emotion, a leather-lung fan shouted from the second balcony, "We love ya Cooz." (Courtesy of the Boston Herald.)

The world champion Celtics are greeted in the Oval Office by Pres. John F. Kennedy on January 31, 1963. From left to right are John Havlicek, trainer Buddy LeRoux, Clyde Lovellette, K. C. Jones, Bob Cousy, Red Auerbach, Jim Loscutoff, President Kennedy, Sam Jones, Frank Ramsey, Tom Heinsohn, and Satch Sanders. (Courtesy of the Doherty family.)

Red Auerbach lectures rookies, from left to right, Ron Bonham, John Thompson, and Bill Vorette at Celtics preseason training camp on September 15, 1964. Both Bonham and Thompson played on two world championship teams before being selected by the Chicago Bulls in the 1966 expansion draft. Thompson later attained hall of fame status as head coach of Georgetown University. (Courtesy of the Sports Museum.)

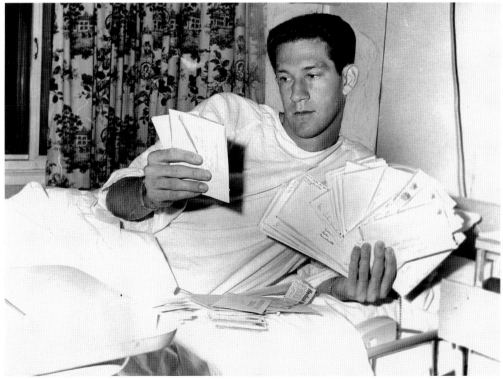

It was broadcaster Curt Gowdy who suggested that Red Auerbach draft a versatile member of the NCAA champion Ohio State named John Havlicek. Within a season of arriving in Boston, the player nicknamed "Hondo" became the logical replacement for Frank Ramsey as the team's indispensable sixth man. He is shown here recovering from surgery in 1964. (Courtesy of the Boston Herald.)

The "Havlicek Stole the Ball" record album was the biggest selling sports highlight record of all time. Among other highlights, it captured the moment on April 15, 1965, made famous by play-by-play announcer Johnny Most's unforgettable radio call, where John Havlicek preserved the Celtics 110-109 victory with a crucial steal of an inbounds pass in the final seconds of the seventh game of the Eastern Conference Finals against Wilt Chamberlain and the hated Philadelphia 76ers.

By the end of his 15th season as head coach, the stress and strain of the job took its toll on the 48-year-old Red Auerbach. During his tenure as head coach and general manager, Auerbach had done everything from drive the team to exhibition games in his station wagon to make hotel reservations while assembling squads he led to nine world championships. The indelible image most fans have of Auerbach is either that of the victorious coach puffing on a cigar or standing on the sideline, forever arguing a call. (Courtesy of the Boston Herald.)

With four minutes remaining in the seventh game of the 1966 NBA Finals, the Celtics led the Lakers by 13 as the Boston Garden crowd waited for Red Auerbach to unwrap and light the final victory cigar of his unrivaled NBA coaching career. Only when the clock ticked down to 16 seconds with a six-point lead did Auerbach gesture to Massachusetts governor John Volpe to light the final cigar. (Photograph by Fred Keenan, courtesy of the Quincy Patriot-Ledger.)

In the spring of 1967, the Celtics had their string of eight straight world titles snapped by the Philadelphia 76ers in a decisive five-game Eastern Conference Final. Player-coach Bill Russell is shown here during a time-out in game two (107-102 loss) at Boston Garden addressing a group that includes Don Nelson (No. 19), K. C. Jones (with a towel), Sam Jones (No. 24), Bailey Howell, Wayne Embry (No. 28), Jim Barnett (No. 11), Satch Sanders (No. 16) and John Havlicek (No. 17). (Courtesy of the Boston Herald.)

With John Havlicek leading the way onto the plane, the Boston Celtics take off for Puerto Rico, where they played a three-game exhibition series with the world champion Philadelphia 76ers in early October 1967. The fans of Puerto Rico saw a preview of the NBA Eastern Conference playoffs in which the Celtics would exact revenge for their defeat the previous season. (Courtesy of the Boston Herald.)

Forward Willie Naulls arrived in Boston from the San Francisco Warriors just prior to the start of the 1963–1964 NBA season. In three seasons in Boston, the former UCLA All-American served as both the backup and replacement for Tom Heinsohn while helping lead the Celtics to world championships in 1963–1964, 1964–1965, and 1965–1966. (Courtesy of the Sports Museum.)

Celtics victory parades, while nowhere near the scale of the recent victory celebrations of the Patriots and Red Sox, were a common sight in Boston in the 1960s. Pictured here on April 26, 1965, are Red Auerbach (in hat puffing a victory cigar) and Tom Heinsohn riding in Mayor John Collins's convertible on Washington Street just below the Old South Meeting House (within a block of Old City Hall). (Courtesy of the Boston Herald.)

Veteran forward Bailey Howell polished his hall of fame credentials in Boston following his arrival in September 1966 via a trade with the Baltimore Bullets in exchange for seven-foot backup center Mel Counts. In four seasons in Boston, Howell was a key contributor to two world championships and averaged exactly 18 points per game to match his uniform number. Howell departed Boston for the Buffalo Braves in the May 1970 expansion draft. (Courtesy of the Sports Museum.)

As the Celtics strung together world championships, their stature in Boston grew steadily during the 1960s. Among their many charitable efforts was support for the Jimmy Fund of the Dana Farber Cancer Institute. Pictured here at a Fenway Park check presentation ceremony is Celtics point guard K. C. Jones with Red Sox legend Ted Williams. (Courtesy of the Sports Museum.)

During the Vietnam era, many professional athletes joined the National Guard, including the Celtics top draft pick in 1966, guard Jim Barnett of Oregon. The Riverside, California, native is shown posing for photographers on August 31, 1966, at Camp Drum, New York, where he trained with the Yankee Division. Following his military training, Barnett managed to play 48 games for the 1966–1967 Celtics before being selected by the San Diego Rockets in the 1967 expansion draft. (Courtesy of the Boston Herald.)

Bill Russell visits former Cleveland Browns star Jim Brown on the set of *Ice Station Zebra* in July 1967. Within two years, Russell joined Brown in retirement. Russell soon found his way to show business where he enjoyed stints as a guest star on *The White Shadow*, *Miami Vice*, and *Saturday Night Live* among other acting roles. Along the way he also coached two other NBA franchises (Seattle SuperSonics and the Sacramento Kings) in addition to serving as color commentator for both ABC and CBS NBA broadcasts. (Courtesy of the Boston Herald.)

Boston Celtics rookie guard Mal Graham sits on his duffel bag on the train platform while waiting for his train to leave for Fort Dix, New Jersey, where he is slated to undergo six months training in the army. The New York University graduate played for two world champions before retiring for health reasons. Following his retirement, Graham scouted Dave Cowens, recommending the Celtics sign the underrated collegian. After completing law school, Graham became a judge, in which capacity he continues to serve the Commonwealth of Massachusetts. He and Dave Cowens also share the distinction of having served as chairs of the Sports Museum in Boston. (Photograph by Michael Shea, courtesy of the Boston Herald.)

The enduring image of Bill Russell as a Celtic is captured in this classic photograph showing the Celtic great battling with Wilt Chamberlain. As with all great sports rivalries, the battles between the Celtics and their rivals of the 1960s—the Warriors, 76ers, and Lakers—was underscored by the individual rivalry between Russell and Chamberlain. The battles fought by Russell and Chamberlain are the essence of Celtics mystique, the triumph of intelligence and heart over sheer talent and brute strength. (Courtesy of the Boston Globe.)

The raising of Celtics world championship banners had become a Boston sports routine throughout the late 1950s and 1960s, as the team captured 11 titles in 13 seasons. (Courtesy of the Boston Herald.)

Celtics player-coach Bill Russell towers over the lectern as he delivers the keynote speech of the evening to members of the graduating class of the Patrick T. Campbell Jr. High School. He urged graduates to respect their white fellow citizens even if they cannot love them. During formal graduation at the Campbell school, a near riot erupted over the presence of Boston school committeewoman Louise Day Hicks. (Courtesy of the Sports Museum.)

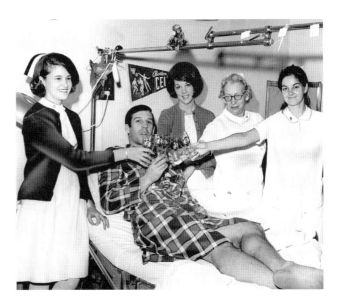

Former Ohio State star Larry Siegfried joined his former college teammate John Havlicek with the Celtics in 1963 and played a part in five world championships before being taken by the Portland Trail Blazers in the 1970 NBA expansion draft. He is pictured here with nurses at St. Elizabeth's Hospital while recovering from a back injury in January 1968. (Courtesy of the Boston Herald.)

Emmette Bryant came to the Celtics from the Phoenix Suns via the Knicks in the summer of 1968. The veteran guard played a key role in the 1968–1969 playoffs as he nearly doubled his regular-season points-per-game average from 5.7 to 11.0 while helping lead Boston to its 11th and most improbable world championship. (Courtesy of the Sports Museum.)

Celtics general manager Red Auerbach pours cream for guard Don Chaney. Chaney, the team's top draft pick from the University of Houston in 1968 (12th overall), became a classic Celtics role player while emerging as one of the best defensive guards in NBA history. In 10 seasons in Boston, he was a member of three world championship teams. (Courtesy of the Sports Museum.)

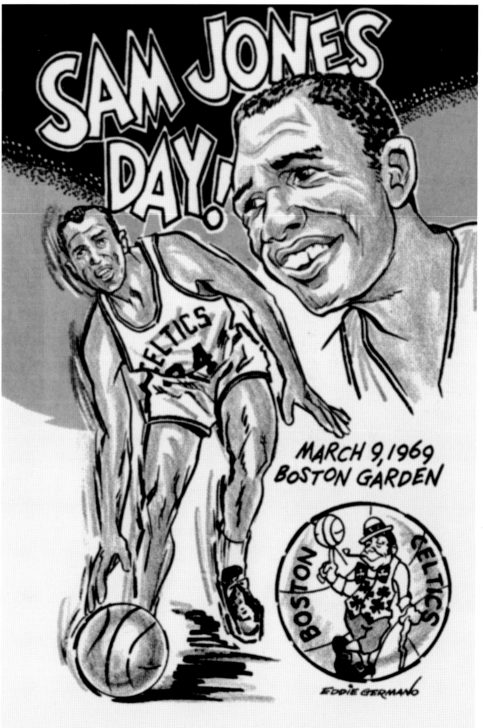

SAM JONES DAY!

MARCH 9, 1969
BOSTON GARDEN

EDDIE GERMANO

Sam Jones was one of many Celtics greats to receive a day in his honor. (Courtesy of the Sports Museum, Flynn Donation.)

Longtime Celtics publicist Howie McHugh served as Walter Brown's right-hand man with the Celtics from the day the franchise was named. McHugh was a staple of the Celtics front office where he was accompanied by his pet cat No Cut. (Photograph by Mike Andersen, courtesy of the *Boston Herald*.)

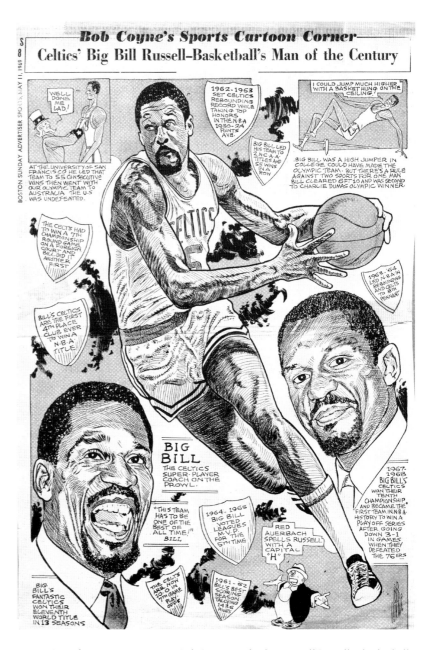

*Boston Record American* cartoonist Bob Coyne paid tribute to Bill Russell as basketball's "Man of the Century." (Courtesy of the Sports Museum, Flynn Donation.)

In a turbulent era of race relations, the Celtics dynasty symbolized the ideal of blacks and whites working together toward a common goal. Red Auerbach is shown with his men, most likely advising them to follow one of his time-honored slogans, "dress British and think Yiddish." (Courtesy of the Boston Herald.)

The public image of Bill Russell was that of a towering enigmatic presence, possessed with greatness and a bit of mystery. For 35¢, Sport magazine attempted to illuminate the myth and the man. (Courtesy of the Sports Museum, Flynn Donation.)

53

The dapper backup forward/center Jim "Bad News" Barnes and his wife walk through City Hall Plaza to a rally and reception for the 1969 world champions held by Mayor Kevin White. In two seasons with the Celtics, Barnes saw limited service before being sold to the Baltimore Bullets just prior to the 1970–1971 season. (Courtesy of the Boston Herald.)

Celtics founder and owner Walter Brown, shown here with the Celtics 1964 draft pick Ron Bonham, was the greatest sportsman in New England history and perhaps the greatest owner in North American professional sports history. He created the Celtics dynasty with an equal lack of capital and ego, instead relying on his intelligence and people skills to attract the likes of Red Auerbach, investor Lou Pieri, and countless others to his cause. His good friend Will Cloney captured Brown's persona when he remarked, "Walter was the most professional amateur I ever knew." (Photograph by Arthur Howard, Boston Sunday Advertiser.)

# THREE

# THE 1970S

On October 23, 1970, the Celtics honored Sam Jones by raising his number to the Boston Garden rafters. Celtics fans harbor fond memories of the sharp-shooting guard whose bank-shot jumpers kissed off the square above the iron with mechanical accuracy. Among his greatest moments was the time he waved a stool at Wilt Chamberlain after some verbal sparring and his last-second clutch shot that won the fourth game of the 1969 finals, tying the series at two games apiece. (Courtesy of the Sports Museum.)

Jacksonville star Rex Morgan was chosen in the second round of the 1970 draft with the 21st overall pick and soon became a cult figure in Boston. His floppy rock star mullet made him a fan favorite for his brief two-season stint in Boston. (Courtesy of the Sports Museum.)

When Dave Cowens was drafted as the fourth overall pick in the 1970 NBA draft (behind Bob Lanier, Rudy Tomjanovich, and Pete Maravich), Celtics fans scratched their heads as Cowens was barely known due to the fact his Florida State team was on NCAA probation and did not take part in any postseason play. Cowens quickly proved to be an excellent selection as he shared Rookie of the Year honors with Geoff Petrie of the Portland Trail Blazers. (Cartoon by Bob Robertson.)

Over the years, the Celtics have made many overseas trips as basketball clinicians and goodwill ambassadors. Several of these trips were sponsored by the U.S. State Department and included excursions to eastern Europe and the Far East. Pictured here are Red Auerbach and John Havlicek on a trip in 1970 with the Burmese Basketball Select Team. (Courtesy of the Sports Museum.)

The tradition of great Celtics shooting guards includes the likes of Bill Sharman, Sam Jones, and Jones's successor JoJo White. Drafted out of the University of Kansas in 1969, White is one of the most underrated players in Celtics history. His quiet demeanor and consistent play was in stark contrast to the flashy styles of the other great guards of his era such as Walt Frazier, Earl "the Pearl" Monroe, and "Pistol" Pete Maravich. (Photograph by Robert Shaver, courtesy of the Sports Museum.)

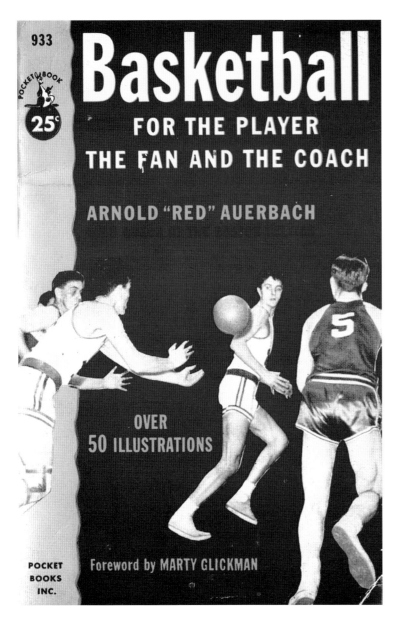

Red Auerbach's *Basketball for the Player, the Fan and the Coach* is one of seven books authored by the Celtics patriarch and has been translated into at least seven languages. It is also the best-selling basketball book of all time and was distributed on each of the team's goodwill tours. (Courtesy of Richard A. Johnson.)

Going skyward is Celtics forward Satch Sanders with Charles Yelverton of Portland in hot pursuit (and with future Celtic Sidney Wicks pulling up short). Note the many empty seats in this game from the 1971–1972 season. The Celtics spotty home attendance from their championship run of the 1960s continued into the 1970s. (Courtesy of the Boston Herald.)

COLLEGE NIGHT

WITH THE

BOSTON CELTICS

WEDNESDAY, NOV. 17, 7:30 p.m.

at BOSTON GARDEN

**HALF PRICE**

See Dave Cowens and the Boston Celtics battle Connie Hawkins and the Phoenix Suns at half price.

**$2.50    $2.00    $1.50    $1.00**

Show your college I.D. card when you purchase tickets at the Boston Garden Box Office and you'll pay half price for $5.00, $4.00, $3.00 and $2.00 seats.

John Havlicek was as versatile a superstar as ever played in the NBA. Adept as either a playmaking guard or small shooting forward, he both outran opponents and controlled the Celtics offense. His career bridged the fast-breaking teams of the Cousy/Russell era to the smart vastly underrated Celtics teams of the 1970s. (Courtesy of the Sports Museum.)

As part of the Celtics' ongoing effort to attract fans, they devised promotions like College Night to draw from the region's many collegians. Invariably the games with the Knicks ended up drawing as many New York fans as Celtics supporters and made for a lively atmosphere. (Courtesy of the Sports Museum, Flynn Donation.)

The 1971–1972 Celtics offered fans a chance to see their heroes as well as stars like Wilt Chamberlain (twice), Clyde Frazier (thrice), Kareem Abdul-Jabbar (twice), and Oscar Robertson (twice), among others, for tickets priced as little as $2 apiece. The Celtics also scheduled four doubleheaders featuring both the Harlem Globetrotters and Fabulous Magicians. (Courtesy of the Sports Museum.)

Dave Cowens extends for a rebound against Artis Gilmore as JoJo White looks on. Cowens, at six feet eight inches, was shorter than most of his fellow centers but more than held his own against the likes of Goliaths like Nate Thurmond, Wilt Chamberlain, Kareem Abdul-Jabbar, and Willis Reed. Cowens's game was complemented by his running speed and endurance, tremendous hustle, and deft shooting touch from the top of the key. He was named NBA Most Valuable Player (MVP) in 1972–1973, one of only four Celtics (along with Cousy, Russell, and Bird) to ever receive the award. (Courtesy of the Sports Museum.)

For many years, Dave Cowens, the most accessible superstar in Boston, rode the Massachusetts Bay Transportation Authority's green line to games at the Boston Garden. His down-home style endeared him to fans who can be seen cheering their hero as he walks to the dressing room following the Celtics 94-78 loss in the seventh game of the 1973 Eastern Division Finals against the Knicks. (Courtesy of the Boston Herald.)

Dave Cowens once said, "Hustle is talent," and for a decade, no player in franchise history ever played every game with as much fire and determination as the redhead from Kentucky. He is pictured here driving against Tom Boerwinkle of the Chicago Bulls. (Courtesy of the Boston Herald.)

Art "Hambone" Williams and Bill Dinwiddie share a laugh prior to Celtics training camp in 1970. Williams spent four seasons with Boston, including the world championship campaign of 1973–1974. Dinwiddie will forever be remembered as the only man ever traded for Bob Cousy, a transaction that occurred when the then Royals coach activated himself in November 1969 and Red Auerbach demanded compensation for the 41-year-old hall of famer. (Courtesy of the Sports Museum.)

Walter Randall served two generations of Celtics players, not only as the team's equipment man, but also as a father-confessor and friend. He was such an ardent and vocal Celtics supporter that he was banned from the Celtics bench following a loud outburst directed against referee Mendy Rudolph. (Courtesy of the Boston Celtics.)

Celtics backup center Hank Finkel drives to the hoop as teammate John Havlicek observes the former Dayton star. Finkel faced the impossible challenge of replacing Bill Russell in the Celtics pivot. Later, as a backup to Dave Cowens, Finkel emerged as a cult hero, and in six seasons, the seven-footer was a member of one world championship team (1974). (Courtesy of the Boston Herald.)

In action from January 30, 1973, Celtics guard Don Chaney outraces New York Knicks hall of fame forward Jerry Lucas to the ball. During the early 1970s, the Celtics-Knicks rivalry was one of the best in NBA history. The Knicks philosophy of "hit the open man" and "dee-fense" was taken straight out of the Celtics basketball gospel by another sharp New Yorker named Red (Holzman). (Courtesy of the Sports Museum.)

In this photograph, three future NBA head coaches converge on a rebound; they are, from left to right, Don Nelson, Paul Silas, and Phil Jackson. Of the three, only Jackson failed to come under the direct influence of Red Auerbach. Auerbach and Jackson are tied for the all-time record for championships as a coach with nine. (Photograph by Pam Schuyler-Cowens, courtesy of the Sports Museum.)

The Celtics' backcourt was bolstered in 1972 when the team selected guard Paul Westphal of the University of Southern California with the 10th overall pick of the draft. Westphal (right), shown here with teammate JoJo White and head coach Tom Heinsohn, spent three seasons in Boston before being traded to the Phoenix Suns for Charlie Scott in May 1975. (Courtesy of the Boston Herald.)

New York Knicks star and future presidential candidate Bill Bradley is sandwiched by John Havlicek (left) and Don Nelson in the opener of the 1972 NBA Eastern Division Finals. The Knicks won this game by a score of 116-94 and went on to capture the series in five games. The series nevertheless served as the coming-out party for a revitalized Celtics franchise that would capture two world titles in the coming four seasons. (Courtesy of the Boston Herald.)

Power forward Paul Silas (No. 35) proved the perfect complement to Dave Cowens in the Celtics' frontcourt following his arrival in Boston via trade from the Phoenix Suns in 1972. Silas's strong, consistent rebounding allowed Cowens greater mobility in and around the key. Silas was a major contributor to the team's 1974 and 1976 world championships, before being traded to Denver just prior to the 1976–1977 season. (Courtesy of the Boston Herald.)

The Celtics of the 1970s were much like the Montreal Canadiens of the 1960s, a mini dynasty within a larger dynastic framework. It is interesting to note that the 1972–1973 team amassed a remarkable regular season record of 68 wins and 14 losses, still the best in Celtics history and among the best in NBA history. That Celtics squad was on track for the title until John Havlicek suffered a shoulder injury in game three of the Eastern Division Finals against the eventual champion New York Knicks. Here Havlicek is shown at the left of a group shot that captures that amazing team. Along with him are Dave Cowens (No. 18), JoJo White (No. 10), and general manager Red Auerbach. (Photograph by Pam Schuyler-Cowens, courtesy of the Sports Museum.)

Paul Westphal drives against Warrior hall of fame forward Rick Barry. In three seasons with the Celtics, Westphal averaged a little over seven points per game, but following his trade to Phoenix, he blossomed into an all-star, averaging 20-plus points. In his first season with the Suns, he helped lead them to a memorable NBA Final against his old teammates. (Courtesy of the Boston Herald.)

*Boston Record American* cartoonist Bob Coyne aptly recognizes John Havlicek's position in the Celtics pantheon. (Courtesy of the Sports Museum, Flynn Donation.)

Celtics forward Dan Nelson battles Knicks forward Bill Bradley before a sold-out Boston Garden. (Courtesy of the Boston Globe.)

Captain John Havlicek runs the Celtics offense as his perennial shadow, former Rhodes Scholar Bill Bradley, works his way up court. The side battles between Havlicek and Bradley were but one facet of the epic battles waged by the Knicks and Celtics during the 1970s. Following Boston's incredible upset of the Knicks in the 1969 Eastern Division Finals, the New Yorkers bested Boston in both the 1972 and 1973 Division Finals before Boston returned the favor on their way to the 1974 world title. (Photograph by Frank O'Brien, courtesy of the Boston Globe.)

Steve Kuberski was one of the few third-round draft choices to ever make the Celtics roster . His rough-and-tumble style endeared him to Boston fans who fondly remembered Bob Brannum and Jim Loscutoff. In eight seasons, he played on two world champions, and he was the last Celtic to wear No. 33 before Larry Bird. (Photograph by Ray Foley, courtesy of the Sports Museum.)

Former North Carolina guard Charlie Scott came to Boston in 1975 in exchange for Paul Westphal and draft choices. In his first season in Boston, Scott teamed with JoJo White to help lead the Celtics to their 13th world championship. He played two more seasons before being traded to the Lakers for Kermit Washington, Don Chaney, and future considerations. (Photograph by Mike Andersen, courtesy of the Boston Herald.)

The indelible image of JoJo White for most Celtics fans was the quick release of his textbook jumper as shown in this home game against the Royals in November 1971. (Photograph by Frank Hill, courtesy of the Sports Museum.)

Since the NBA started naming all-defensive teams in 1969, only one Celtic has been named to the team as many as eight times: John Havlicek. Hondo's fitness and athleticism were legendary, having once earned him a tryout as wide receiver for the Cleveland Browns and several visits from major-league baseball scouts. He is shown here escorting Mike Riordan of the Baltimore Bullets to the Boston Garden baseline in playoff action from May 1975. (Photograph by Frank O'Brien, courtesy of the Boston Globe.)

Basketball's reigning redheads battle it out at Boston Garden. Both Bill Walton and Dave Cowens (No. 18) march to the proverbial different drummer and both were fiery competitors who won MVP awards, led their teams to world championships, and had their careers shortened by debilitating injuries. (Photograph by Pamela Scuyler-Cowens, courtesy of the photographer.)

# Celtics win, 128-126—in triple OT

The fifth game of the 1976 NBA Finals has been called by many the greatest game in NBA history. In an epic battle that featured a brawl between a fan and referee Richie Powers, several unheralded Celtics played starring roles, including benchwarmer Glenn McDonald, who scored six overtime points to help lead Boston to victory in the third overtime. Pictured here is the Boston Globe sports page proclaiming the victory. (Courtesy of the Boston Globe.)

Super sub Glenn McDonald enjoyed the game of a lifetime after being pressed into service in the final stages of the epic triple-overtime win over the Suns. McDonald is shown making two vital free throws in the third overtime period to help secure the win. (Courtesy of the Sports Museum.)

The 1976 world champions are guests of Mayor Kevin White at a city hall reception. The players are, from left to right, (first row) Jim Ard, Jerome Anderson, Glenn McDonald, and Kevin Stacom; (second row) Dave Cowens, Paul Silas, JoJo White, John Havlicek, Don Nelson, Charlie Scott, Steve Kuberski, and Tom Boswell. (Courtesy of the Sports Museum.)

No Celtics championship faded faster than the 1976 title after Curtis Rowe (left) and his former college teammate Sidney Wicks (not pictured) came to town. Both arrived with great expectations and fell far short of delivering the goods. Pictured with Rowe is rookie Jeff Judkins, who joined the team as the Celtics second-round pick in 1978. (Photograph by Tom Tajima, courtesy of the Boston Herald.)

Sidney Wicks grabs a rebound against the Buffalo Braves while surrounded by teammates JoJo White (No. 10), Fred Saunders (No. 20), Dave Cowens (No. 18), and John Havlicek. (Photograph by Mike Andersen, courtesy of the Boston Herald.)

Former UCLA teammates Dave Meyers (left) and Sidney Wicks square off at Boston Garden in 1978. In two seasons with the Celtics, Wicks's inconsistent play helped make him a symbol of the team's faded glory. (Photograph by Mike Andersen, courtesy of the Boston Herald.)

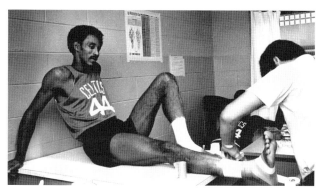

Hall of fame guard Dave Bing played his final season with the Celtics in 1977–1978 after being signed as a free agent from the Washington Bullets. The 34-year-old played in 80 games before retiring at season's end. (Photograph by Paul Benoit, courtesy of the Boston Herald.)

Local favorite Ernie DiGregorio returned to New England as a free agent five years after having captured NBA Rookie of the Year honors. In limited service, DiGregorio played the last 27 games of his NBA career an hour up the road from his hometown of Providence, Rhode Island. (Courtesy of the Boston Globe.)

Red Auerbach searches for matches to light his cigar as team owner John Y. Brown gazes at new Celtics signing and former Providence College star Marvin Barnes. Barnes came to Boston in a blockbuster deal with the San Diego Clippers on August 4, 1978, that also brought Billy Knight, Nate Archibald, and draft picks in exchange for Sidney Wicks, Kermit Washington, Kevin Kunnert, and the rights to Freeman Williams. (Courtesy of the Boston Herald.)

Satch Sanders is shown in front of his restaurant in the Back Bay a couple of years after his short stint as Celtics head coach in 1978. Sanders, a lover of books and jazz, had also coached at Harvard and would soon help found the Center for the Study of Sport in Society at Northeastern University. (Courtesy of the Sports Museum.)

Dave Cowens looks wistful as he leaves the court following his first game as player-coach of the Celtics, a winning effort against the Denver Nuggets on November 17, 1978. The nightmare year would continue, as Boston finished last for the first time since the 1949–1950 season. (Photograph by Mike Andersen, courtesy of the Boston Herald.)

Former Villanova star Chris Ford hit the first three-point basket in NBA history and finished the 1979–1980 season as the league's second-best long-distance shooter behind Seattle's "Downtown" Freddie Brown. For four seasons, he was paired in the Celtics backcourt with hall of famer Tiny Archibald and helped lead the Celtics to the 1981 world championship. In 1990, he became the sixth former Celtics player named as the team's head coach. (Courtesy of the Sports Museum.)

# THE 1980S

Larry Bird was viewed by many as the "hick from French Lick." It was an identity the superstar embraced so that his opponents would underestimate his extraordinary intelligence and court sense. It also proved a lucrative persona, as Bird was content to portray himself as a simple country boy in countless advertisements, including the filming of the "Choose Your Weapons" advertisement for Converse. (Courtesy of the Boston Herald.)

**LARRY BIRD**

The arrival of Larry Bird in 1979 represented nothing less than a complete revitalization of the franchise. The same season, Magic Johnson was making his debut with the Lakers, and soon both players elevated the entire NBA. For his part, Bird helped lead the Celtics to the greatest single-season turnaround in NBA history as Boston went from last place in the 1978–1979 season to first place and a record of 61 wins and 21 losses in the 1979–1980 season. (Courtesy of the Sports Museum.)

Former Louisiana State University standout "Pistol" Pete Maravich arrived in Boston in January 1980 after being waived by the Utah Jazz. Maravich teamed with fellow hall of famers Dave Cowens and Larry Bird in the final season of his illustrious career. (Courtesy of the Boston Globe).

From left to right, Tracy Jackson, Terry Duerod, and Charles Bradley grab some pine on the Celtics bench in November 1981. During the championship campaign of 1980–1981, Duerod achieved folk-hero status, with fans shouting "Doooooo" at the end of games as they anticipated his patented long-range jump shots. Both Bradley and Jackson were selected in the 1981 draft with the 23rd and 25th overall picks, respectively. Jackson played just 11 games before being sold to the Bulls, while Bradley played two full seasons before being waived in 1983. (Photograph by Mike Andersen, courtesy of the Boston Herald.)

Nate "Tiny" Archibald was the Celtics' flashiest and most talented point guard since Bob Cousy. He also enjoyed great success at the end of his career, leading the Celtics to a playoff record of 26 wins and 18 losses in the four seasons from 1979–1980 to 1982–1983. Included in this run was the 1981 world championship and a painful seven-game loss to Philadelphia in which Archibald's injury likely cost the Celtics the series and a chance to defend their title. (Courtesy of the Sports Museum.)

The Celtics were much like the New York Yankees in that they were the team that attracted older superstars seeking an elusive world championship ring. Such was the case with Nate Archibald, who finally got his wish in 1981. He is pictured holding the NBA's Larry O'Brien Trophy aloft at the rally held at city hall in honor of the 1981 champions. (Photograph by Stanley Forman, courtesy of the Boston Herald.)

In 1981, the Celtics gambled with their third draft choice, the 31st pick in the second round, and selected Brigham Young guard Danny Ainge despite the fact Ainge was playing major-league baseball with the Toronto Blue Jays at the time. Following a reported payment of $800,000 to the Blue Jays in the fall of 1981, Ainge arrived in Boston and promptly signed a five-year contract with the Celtics. Ainge and son Austin are shown on the Celtics bench. (Photograph by William Polo, courtesy of the Boston Herald.)

Cedric "Cornbread" Maxwell owned the distinction of playing with John Havlicek as a teammate and against Michael Jordan as an opponent. Maxwell arrived in Boston just as the Celtics started a tailspin. His individual career blossomed, however, and team success soon came with the arrival of Larry Bird, Robert Parish, and Kevin McHale by 1980. (Photograph by William Polo, courtesy of the Boston Herald.)

On June 9, 1980, Red Auerbach executed the second-greatest transaction in franchise history (after the Bill Russell deal) by trading two first-round picks (including the top pick) in the 1980 NBA draft to the Golden State Warriors for center Robert Parish and the third pick in the 1980 draft, which the Celtics used to pick Kevin McHale. In Boston, Parish blossomed into an all-star. He is pictured here in the 1985 NBA Finals shooting over Kareem Abdul-Jabbar. (Photograph by Barry Chin, courtesy of the Boston Herald.)

Bill Fitch (right) was a taskmaster in the mold of former Red Sox manager Dick Williams. In two seasons, he led the Celtics from last place to their first NBA title in six years with a cast that included future hall of famers such as Nate Archibald, Larry Bird, Kevin McHale, and Robert Parish. In four seasons, Fitch led the team to a combined regular season record of 242 wins and 86 losses—a .738 winning percentage—while capturing the 1981 NBA title. (Courtesy of the Boston Globe.)

Celtics radio broadcaster Johnny Most's raspy voice and passionate, sometimes manic, play-calling were team trademarks. In his self-described perch "high above courtside," Most started every broadcast by telling fans the Celtics were about to do "basketball battle." For nearly four decades, Most ignored objectivity while describing opponents as gutless whiners among other insults and delighting Celtics fans in the process. (Courtesy of the Boston Herald.)

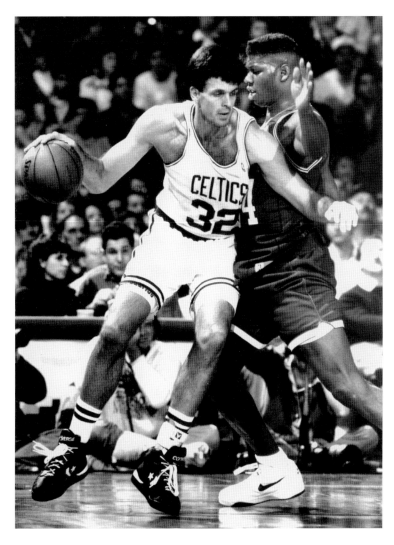

Celtics forward Kevin McHale has been described as the greatest low-post player of all time. His corkscrew gyrations and deft shooting touch left most opponents talking to themselves. As both a starter and sixth man, McHale was a superb scorer, finishing his career as the Celtics' fourth leading scorer with 17,335 points. (Courtesy of the Sports Museum.)

Celtics forward Cedric Maxwell helped lead Boston to an incredible comeback against the rival 76ers in the 1981 Eastern Conference Finals, as the Celtics clawed their way back from a 3-1 game deficit to win the final three games by margins of two, two, and one points. Maxwell is shown here dunking over Sixer Andrew Toney. (Courtesy of the Sports Museum.)

Nate Archibald nurses his dislocated shoulder as he watches the Celtics lose a heartbreaking seven-game Eastern Conference Final to the 76ers on May 23, 1982. The future hall of famer injured his shoulder in the third game of the series and did not return to action until the following season. (Courtesy of the Boston Herald.)

K. C. Jones (left) and Red Auerbach beam at the announcement of Jones being named the ninth coach in franchise history on June 7, 1983. In his five-season tenure, Jones led the team to world championships in 1984 and 1986 and achieved the best winning percentage of any Celtics coach with a .751 mark (308-102). (Photograph by Jim Mahoney, courtesy of the Boston Herald.)

GREG KITE

Greg Kite was a banger in the best Celtics tradition of Bob Brannum, Jim Loscutoff, Steve Kuberski, and Dave Cowens. A first-round draft pick in 1983 (21st overall), Kite played four and a half seasons with Boston while serving as Robert Parish's backup on two world championship teams. (Courtesy of the Sports Museum.)

In 1974, a raw young forward named Michael Leon Carr signed with the world champion Celtics on October 10 only to be waived five days later. In 1980, that forward came back to Boston as M. L. Carr, signing as a free agent. Soon he became a crowd favorite with his hustle and overall enthusiasm. His trademark was his towel-waving cheerleading that soon became as much a Celtics symbol as Red Auerbach's cigar. (Photograph by Mike Andersen, courtesy of the Boston Herald.)

Guard Quinn Buckner arrived in Boston in 1982 in a trade that sent the rights to future hall of famer Dave Cowens to the Milwaukee Bucks. Buckner proved a perfect fit for the Celtics as Nate Archibald was coming to the end of his career in Boston and rookie Danny Ainge was slowly learning his trade. Buckner was a solid contributor for the 1984 world champions while coming off the bench. Eventually Boston traded him to Indiana in 1985. (Courtesy of the Boston Globe.)

Gerald Henderson, pictured here in action against the Bucks, became a Boston sports legend in 1984. With 13 seconds to go in the second game of the 1984 NBA Finals, the Celtics were close to falling to a two-game deficit to the Lakers when Henderson stole a James Worthy pass and scored a layup that sent the game into overtime. The Celtics went on to win the game and the hard-fought seven-game series for their 15th NBA crown. (Photograph by Jim Mahoney, courtesy of the Boston Herald.)

M. L. Carr hams it up with the Larry O'Brien Trophy in the Celtics locker room following Boston's 111-102 victory over Los Angeles in game seven at Boston Garden in 1984. The third figure from the left in the background is reigning world middleweight champion Marvelous Marvin Hagler. (Courtesy of the Sports Museum.)

Once again, Carr grabs the spotlight as the Celtics celebrate their 1984 world championship with yet another celebration on City Hall Plaza. (Courtesy of the Boston Herald.)

**SCOTT WEDMAN**

Scott Wedman proved a versatile acquisition by the Celtics, who used him as both a guard and small forward. An introspective vegetarian, Wedman saw a lot of action off the bench for the world champions of 1984 and 1986. (Courtesy of the Sports Museum.)

Reserve guard Rick Carlisle beat considerable odds to make the roster of the defending world champions as a third-round draft pick (70th overall) out of the University of Virginia in 1984. Carlisle was a bit of a renaissance man as he was a skilled jazz pianist and student of the game. He captured a championship ring in 1986 and has since made a career as one of the NBA's best coaches. (Courtesy of the Boston Herald.)

Larry Bird once called Dennis Johnson the best player
he had ever played with, high praise from one of the best
players in NBA history. Johnson, a superb defensive player
and playmaker, came to Boston in a trade for backup center
Rick Robey and draft choices. Johnson arrived just as Nate
Archibald was waived by Boston. He soon became the
driving wheel for one of the greatest Celtics teams ever. He is
shown here battling Alvin Robertson of the Spurs. (Courtesy
of the Boston Herald.)

The big three of Kevin McHale, Robert Parish, and Larry Bird filled the Boston Garden for a dozen seasons, leading the Celtics to world championships in 1981, 1984, and 1986. The formidable frontcourt trio is generally regarded as the greatest in the history of the sport. (Photograph by Tom Miller, courtesy of the photographer.)

The 1986 Celtics featured a roster that included four hall of famers (Bird, Bill Walton, McHale, and Parish) and one player who will certainly be named in the future (Dennis Johnson). Walton (left), pictured here with Kevin McHale, was obtained by general manager Jan Volk in a trade with the Los Angeles Clippers. With Boston, Walton became the tallest sixth man in history and helped lead one of the greatest teams in NBA history to their 16th world championship. (Courtesy of the Sports Museum.)

Coach K. C. Jones directs the Celtics in practice. His 1985–1986 squad finished the regular season with an incredible home record of 40-1 and won a total of 67 regular-season games before taking the world championship with a 15-3 won/lost record in the playoffs. (Courtesy of the Boston Globe.)

**JERRY SICHTING**

Backup guard Jerry Sichting proved a steal when traded to the Celtics by the Pacers just prior to the start of the 1985–1986 season for a second-round draft choice. (Courtesy of the Sports Museum.)

It took Boston fans nearly 40 years to fully appreciate the glorious dynasty in their midst. *Boston Globe* columnist Bob Ryan said it best when he remarked, "Other teams have a history, the Celtics have a mystique." (Photograph by Arthur Pollock, courtesy of the Boston Herald.)

Danny Ainge grimaces after taking a fall during game seven of the 1987 Eastern Conference Finals against the Pistons at Boston Garden. This series was the last blaze of glory for the Celtics' 1980s dynasty. The Celtics came back to beat the upstart Pistons in a dramatic seven games before losing to their rivals from Los Angeles in six games. (Photograph by William Polo, courtesy of the Boston Herald.)

Celtics fans can only dream of how well Bird and Havlicek would have played had they had a chance to collaborate. Unfortunately Hondo retired one year before Bird arrived in town. Here the two Celtics legends share a moment on the Boston Garden parquet in April 1987. (Photograph by Ted Fitzgerald, courtesy of the Boston Herald.)

In 1987, the Celtics drafted local hero Reggie Lewis (left) with the 22nd overall pick of the draft and seven-foot center Brad Lohaus with the 45th pick. In two seasons with Boston, Lohaus saw limited action as backup to Robert Parish while Lewis developed into a sharp-shooting forward who eventually succeeded Larry Bird as Celtics captain in 1993. (Photograph by Jim Davis, courtesy of the Boston Herald.)

In 1988, the Sports Museum honored Larry Bird with the unveiling of a life-size wooden sculpture by renowned artist Armand LaMontagne. Shown with Bird at the private unveiling ceremony at Boston's Ritz Hotel are Red Auerbach and Bird's mother, Georgia. (Courtesy of the Sports Museum.)

Former Arkansas star Joe Kleine arrived in 1988 as the latest backup for Robert Parish. His Celtics career lasted five seasons before the team decided not to renew his contract in 1993. (Courtesy of the Sports Museum.)

Former Boston College star John Bagley played a little over two seasons with the Celtics following his trade by the New Jersey Nets. Often injured, he was forced to sit out the entire 1990–1991 season. He is pictured here making a pass behind the back of Bucks center Jack Sikma. (Courtesy of the Sports Museum.)

Celtics general manager Jan Volk welcomes Croatian forward Dino Radja to the Celtics on the occasion of his selection as the 40th overall pick in the 1989 NBA draft. After playing in Italy for three seasons, Radja finally made his Celtics debut in 1993 and became a solid player for Boston for four seasons, during which time he averaged 16.7 points per game. Volk, a native of Newton, served the Celtics for nearly three decades and was general manager of the 1984 and 1986 world champions. (Courtesy of the Sports Museum.)

# THE 1990S

Starting in the late 1980s, Larry Bird experienced back problems, which escalated into a chronic condition that kept him on the sidelines for virtually the entire 1988–1989 season. For his final three seasons (1990–1992), he played an average of 60 games per season, many of which ended up being heroic endurance tests for the injured superstar. (Courtesy of the Sports Museum.)

The Celtics bid farewell to all-star guard Dennis Johnson following the end of the 1990 season, when he retired at age 35. In seven seasons with the Celtics, Johnson was named to three NBA All-Defense teams and helped lead the Celtics to world championships in 1984 and 1986. (Photograph by William Polo, courtesy of the Boston Herald.)

Trainer Ed Lacerte checks on Brian Shaw on the Boston Garden sidelines in 1991. Shaw, the team's first-round pick in 1988 (24th overall), had an excellent rookie season and was named to the NBA Rookie All-Star Second Team. However, Shaw soon wore out his welcome with the Celtics when his agent, Jerome Stanley, took public potshots at team management. In January 1992, he was traded to the Miami Heat for guard Sherman Douglas. (Photograph by Mike Adaskeveg, courtesy of the Boston Herald.)

Celtics president Red Auerbach relaxes with a cigar at a 1991 Celtics practice at Brandeis University as Kevin McHale prepares to take the court. By the early 1990s, the Celtics dynasty had started to fade, and tragedies like the death of draft pick Len Bias haunted a franchise seeking a return to glory. McHale fell victim to nagging leg injuries and retired following the 1992–1993 season. (Courtesy of the Sports Museum.)

Kevin McHale's fadeaway jumper was the NBA's most unstoppable shot since Kareem Abdul-Jabbar's skyhook. On March 3, 1985, McHale torched the Pistons for a then Celtics individual game-scoring high of 56 points in a 138-129 victory. Nine days later, Larry Bird kidded McHale following his 60-point effort against the Atlanta Hawks in New Orleans. Both marks remain the top two individual single-game point totals in team history. (Photograph by Ted Fitzgerald, courtesy of the Boston Herald.)

In the fifth and decisive game of the Celtics first-round playoff series with the Pacers in 1991, Larry Bird contributed one of his all-time best, and most dramatic, performances. After he had injured his back diving for a ball in the first half, Bird returned midway through the third quarter to thunderous applause at the Boston Garden. In 12 minutes, Bird scored 14 points and dished out three assists in helping lead Boston to a 124-121 victory. (Courtesy of the Boston Herald.)

Celtics guard Dee Brown made headlines upon his arrival in Boston in 1990 for both good and bad reasons. In a well-publicized incident, Wellesley police mistook him for a criminal suspect and questioned him at gunpoint in a manner that led many to accuse them justly of random racial profiling. On a more positive note, Brown won the 1991 All-Star Game Slam Dunk Contest after memorably pumping up his Reebok sneakers prior to his winning jam. (Courtesy of the Sports Museum.)

John Bagley's position and expression sums up the team's place in the standings and fans' deflated expectations after the Celtics were eliminated in the first round of the 1993 playoffs by the Charlotte Hornets by a three-games-to-one margin. (Courtesy of the Sports Museum.)

Former Syracuse star Sherman Douglas showed glimpses of the potential he showed in college while playing for the Celtics from 1991 to 1996. Plagued by weight problems and inconsistent performances, Douglas had his best season for Boston in the 1994–1995 season, when he helped lead the Celtics to a first-round playoff date with Shaquille O'Neal and the Orlando Magic. (Courtesy of the Boston Celtics.)

Northeastern University product Reggie Lewis proved a shrewd draft choice for the Celtics in 1987. Over several seasons, Lewis evolved from an eager benchwarmer to a star in the making. Not only did Lewis earn a place on the East roster at the 1992 All-Star Game but later that season was named captain of the Celtics. (Photograph by Steve Lipofsky, courtesy of the photographer.)

Reggie Lewis sits on the Boston Garden parquet following his sudden collapse in the Celtics opening playoff game against the Charlotte Hornets on April 29, 1993. For three months afterward, Lewis was repeatedly examined by teams of physicians of both his and the Celtics' choosing who debated his basketball future. Sadly the Celtics captain died after suffering heart failure following another collapse while playing pickup basketball at Brandeis University on July 27, 1993. (Photograph by Bill Belknap, courtesy of the Boston Herald.)

Four-year-old Cassim Morris of Boston hides his sadness as he stands outside Matthews Arena at Northeastern University as a long line of mourners makes its way into the arena for the funeral of Reggie Lewis on August 2, 1993. (Photograph by Lisa Bul, courtesy of the Boston Herald.)

Former Providence College basketball coach and Big East Conference founder Dave Gavitt (right) came to the Celtics in 1990 as senior executive vice president of basketball operations. He is pictured talking to head coach Chris Ford at practice in 1991. Under Gavitt's direction, the Celtics made the playoffs during the first three of his four years with the team. (Photograph by Mike Adaskaveg, courtesy of the Boston Herald.)

On the day after his funeral, fans left flowers and mementos at the grave site of Reggie Lewis at Jamaica Plain's Forest Hills Cemetery. (Photograph by Arthur Pollock, courtesy of the Boston Herald.)

Following his retirement in 1992, Celtics legend Larry Bird joined the team's brain trust as a special assistant. He is shown here with former teammate and Celtics director of basketball operations M. L. Carr (left) and senior executive vice president Dave Gavitt at the Celtics' Brandeis University practice site in 1995. (Courtesy of the Sports Museum.)

In 1991, the Celtics made University of North Carolina star Rick Fox their first-round draft choice with the 24th overall pick. Fox soon paid dividends as he was chosen to the 1992 NBA All-Rookie Second Team. In 1996, he was named the Celtics' 10th captain, succeeding the duo of Dominique Wilkins and Dee Brown. (Photograph by Jim Davis, courtesy of the Boston Herald.)

In the summer of 1994, the Celtics signed free agent point guard David Wesley. The six-foot-tall Baylor product soon became a crowd favorite with his sharp passing and up-tempo game. His career took off following his move to the Charlotte Hornets via free agency in 1997. (Courtesy of the Boston Herald.)

Celtics head coach M. L. Carr presided over some of the worst teams in recent memory. His cumulative record over two seasons was 48-116, which accounted for the worst-ever win percentage for a Celtics head coach at .293. Included in this run was the abysmal 15-67 season of 1996–1997. (Courtesy of the Boston Herald.)

Boston College star Dana Barros came to the Celtics in 1995 as an unrestricted free agent after having spent the first six years of his career divided between four seasons with the SuperSonics and two with the 76ers. Known primarily as a skilled long-range shooter, Barros set an NBA record on January 10, 1996, when he scored a three-point basket in his 89th consecutive game. It was one of the few highlights for the last-place team. (Courtesy of the Sports Museum.)

Celtics fans had high hopes for Ron Mercer when the Kentucky star was drafted by Boston with one of the team's two first-round picks (Chauncy Billups was the other first-round pick) in the 1997 draft. Not only was Mercer playing for his college mentor, newly hired Celtics coach Rick Pitino, but he ended up playing his way onto the first team of the Schick Rookie All-Stars. However, after two seasons in Boston, he was dealt with Popeye Jones and Dwayne Schintzius to the Denver Nuggets for Danny Fortson, Eric Williams, Eric Washington, and a first-round draft choice. (Courtesy of Sports Action Images.)

After Antoine Walker scored the second-highest point total for a Celtics rookie with 1,435 points (Larry Bird holds the rookie record with 1,745 points) in the horrible 1996–1997 season, fans prayed for a franchise comeback based on the combination of his skills with those of the Celtics' hoped-for lottery pick of Tim Duncan. When the lottery did not swing Boston's way, Walker shouldered the burden as Boston's star leading the team in points, rebounds, steals, and double-doubles. (Courtesy of Sports Action Images.)

The press conference heralding the arrival of Rick Pitino in May 1997 as Celtics president and head coach was presented with as much fanfare as any such announcement in recent Boston sports history. Great expectations followed after Pitino's Celtics shocked the Bulls with an opening night defeat. It would prove the high-water mark of Pitino's three-and-a-half-season stint, during which time the team never made the playoffs. Pitino resigned as president and head coach midway through the 2001 season. (Courtesy of Sports Action Images.)

The Celtics called Boston Garden home for 49 seasons, starting in 1946–1947 and ending with the closing of the arena in 1994–1995. During that time, they embraced the many charms and quirks of the building, such as the famed, but creaky parquet floor, the lack of air-conditioning, and the intimate confines that had fans serving as the Celtics' sixth man. Opposing coaches loved to hate the building and sometimes blamed it as much as the referees or Celtics for their team's misfortunes. (Courtesy of the Sports Museum.)

No player symbolized the malaise of the 1990s more than center Pervis Ellison. The former University of Louisville star came to the Celtics as Robert Parish's replacement via unrestricted free agency in 1994. During his six years with the Celtics, Ellison spent much of his time on the disabled list, including missing the entire 1998–1999 season. He averaged slightly less than 40 games per season for the five in which he did play. (Courtesy of the Boston Herald.)

Celtics fans mourned the closing and demolition of the Boston Garden in the late 1990s. Their spirit is captured in the antics of this rabid fan, posed outside the Boston Garden entrance in 1984. (Courtesy of the Boston Herald.)

# FROM 2000

When venture capitalist Wyc Grousbeck led a group that purchased the Celtics in 2001, he became the first team chief executive to hail from Greater Boston since team founder Walter Brown. Grousbeck, a former national collegiate rowing champion at Princeton, has made the winning of Banner 17 the mission of his management team. (Courtesy of the Boston Celtics.)

Point guard Kenny Anderson directed the Celtics for four and a half seasons following his trade from the Toronto Raptors in 1998. His finest hour for Boston came in the spring of 2003 when he led the Celtics to playoff series wins over the 76ers and Pistons on the way to an inspired but losing effort against the Nets in the Eastern Conference Finals. (Courtesy of the Boston Celtics.)

Mark Blount was the Celtics' main man under the basket in his five full seasons with the team. He excelled at shot blocking, reaching 76 in his rookie year of 2000–2001, the highest total by a Celtics rookie since Kevin McHale back in 1980–1981. Blount also was a force in the offensive part of the game as well, averaging 2.5 offensive rebounds per game in the 2003–2004 campaign. (Courtesy of Sports Action Images.)

Paul Pierce was the star of his team while playing at Kansas, earning the MVP award in Big 12 tournament play in both 1997 and 1998. His success continued in the NBA, earning a unanimous selection to the 1998–1999 Schick All-Rookie First Team. Pierce proved his accomplishments were far from a fluke in the 2000–2001 season by becoming the first Celtic since Larry Bird in 1988 to reach the 2,000-point mark for one season, with 2,071. (Courtesy of Sports Action Images.)

Often referred to simply and lovingly as "Waltah" by Celtics broadcaster Tommy Heinsohn after knocking down a big three-pointer, Walter McCarty was a crowd favorite. With the exception of his rookie year, McCarty never started more than 23 games in a season throughout his eight-year Celtics career, but he made his share of big plays and earned more than a few "Tommy Points." (Courtesy of Sports Action Images.)

Center Tony Battie came to Boston in a trade from the rarest of Boston trading partners, the Los Angeles Lakers. In an exchange of centers, Boston sent Travis Knight westward for the six-foot-eleven-inch Battie. In six seasons with Boston, Battie showed flashes of promise but mostly was a journeyman averaging but 6.8 points per game. (Courtesy of Sports Action Images.)

For nearly a quarter century, former Celtics great Tommy Heinsohn (left) and Dorchester native Mike Gorman have served as the television voices of the Celtics, first on Sports Channel and currently on Fox Sports Net. They are one of the best broadcasting teams in the business, with Gorman's sharp play-by-play offset by Heinsohn's passionate color commentary. Heinsohn's style is loved by Celtics fans nostalgic for the home-slanted interpretative skills akin to those of the late great Johnny Most. (Courtesy of Fox Sports Net New England.)

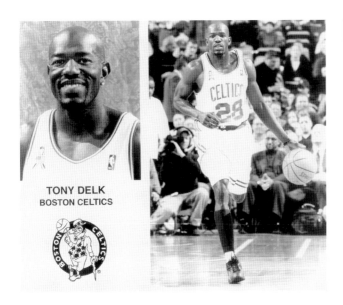

Guard Tony Delk just missed playing for Rick Pitino, his former coach at the University of Kentucky, when he came to Boston along with Rodney Rodgers in a trade with Phoenix for Randy Brown, Milt Palacio, Joe Johnson, and a 2002 first-round draft pick. Delk never quite lived up to his collegiate stardom in Boston while playing inconsistently in his two seasons with the Celtics. (Courtesy of the Boston Celtics.)

Jim O'Brien arrived in Boston in 1997 as an assistant to then head coach Rick Pitino. Following Pitino's resignation on January 8, 2001, O'Brien was first named interim head coach before being hired full-time later that spring. In his two full seasons at the helm of the Celtics, he led them to consecutive playoff appearances, including a surprise appearance in the Eastern Conference against the Nets in 2003. (Courtesy of Sports Action Images.)

Russian center Vitaly Potapenko not only looked like the villain in a James Bond film, he also played tough while scoring an average of 7.5 points per game over his four seasons in Boston. (Courtesy of the Boston Globe.)

Jiri Welsch, a Czech-born forward, started his professional basketball playing career at the tender age of 17 in Europe. After five seasons of playing in Europe, Welsch made his way to the United States and was drafted 16th overall in the 2002 entry draft by Philadelphia. The Celtics picked him up in a trade with the Dallas Mavericks and put this hustling player to work, starting in 100 of his games in his two full seasons wearing Celtics green. (Courtesy of Sports Action Images.)

The year 1996 was a good year for Antoine Walker. Only a few months after winning the NCAA title with the Kentucky Wildcats, he then got drafted sixth overall by the Celtics. Walker soon teamed up with Paul Pierce, and they gave the Celtics a formidable all-star one-two punch. Walker and Pierce led several very good Boston teams, including the memorable 2001–2002 squad, which ended with the Celtics falling short 4-2 against the Nets in the Eastern Conference Finals, despite the heroic efforts of Walker. (Courtesy of Sports Action Images.)

Raef LaFrentz is the Celtics go-to big man under the net, with a career average of 11.3 points per game. He is also an impressive shot-blocker, finishing the 2001–2002 NBA season averaging 2.73 blocks per game, ranked second in the league. LaFrentz's outside shooting touch also makes him especially tough to defend. (Courtesy of Sports Action Images.)

The old greets the new as Celtics president Red Auerbach, who has been part of the Celtics organization for 56 years and is owner of 16 championship rings, and Doc Rivers meet prior to a team practice. Rivers, with a career-winning percentage of .501, with the Orlando Magic and Boston, hopes to connect with his youthful team and help Auerbach get a 17th ring. (Courtesy of Sports Action Images.)

Gary Payton was traded to Boston in his 15th year in the NBA and had already been well known for his deserved nickname, "the Glove." From 1994 to 2001, Payton was named to the All-Defensive First Team and received the Defensive Player of the Year award in 1996. Payton could also score, reaching the 20,000-career-point mark with the Celtics on November 10, 2004, in a game against Portland. (Courtesy of Sports Action Images.)

Ricky Davis bounced around three teams in his first six years in the NBA before arriving to Boston. His talent was undeniable, but his character was questionable after acts such as shooting on his own basket to get a rebound in his attempts of a triple-double. But the Celtics were a good fit for Davis to be a key role player, averaging 16 points per game in the 2004–2005 season, while only starting in 11 of 82 games that season. (Courtesy of Sports Action Images.)

Marcus Banks was acquired by Boston after the speedy guard was available after being drafted by Memphis, with the 13th overall draft selection in 2003. Banks was a solid player off the bench his two full years with the Celtics, having a constant .400 field-goal percentage. He was then traded along with Ricky Davis, Mark Blount, and Justin Reed to the Timberwolves. (Courtesy of Sports Action Images.)

While at Oklahoma State, guard Tony Allen earned the honor of Big 12 Player of the Year for the 2003–2004 season, which led to his even bigger accomplishment of being drafted 25th in the first round of the NBA entry draft by Boston. Allen is battling for playing time on the deep Celtics roster and has developed his abilities under coach Doc Rivers. (Courtesy of Sports Action Images.)

Tom Gugliotta came a long way before signing with the Celtics in 2004. He lived up to his status as the sixth overall draft pick in 1992 by averaging over 17 points per game in three of his first six seasons. Boston was his sixth NBA team, and as his playing time shrunk, he still proved valuable as both a role player and solid influence on younger players. (Courtesy of Sports Action Images.)

Justin Reed enjoyed an impressive collegiate career at Ole Miss, receiving All–Southeastern Conference honors each of his four years and ranking fifth in all-time scoring as a Rebel. He only played in 23 games his rookie season for Boston and in 2005 was traded from the Celtics in a deal with the Timberwolves. (Courtesy of Sports Action Images.)

Drafted 24th overall by Boston, Delonte West was a superb candidate to lead a young but talented Celtics team. Delonte came from a winning tradition, being one half of the impressive backcourt at St. Joseph's, which had an undefeated regular season (27-00) and a 30-2 overall record. His success has already begun to show at the professional level, becoming a regular starter in the 2005–2006 season and averaging nearly 12 points per game. (Courtesy of Sports Action Images.)

Al Jefferson skipped college in favor of the NBA and got the Celtics' attention; they drafted him with their first-round selection in 2004. He provides Boston with youth, size, and strength. In the space of a year, Jefferson went from worrying about the size of his prom tuxedo to concerning himself with playoff matchups. (Courtesy of Sports Action Images.)

In the spring of 2005, Boston fans felt the Celtics had regained some of their postseason magic with an impressive win against Indiana in opening game of the first round of the Eastern Conference playoffs. Not only had Antoine Walker returned to Boston, but both he and veteran Paul Pierce worked well with a young team that had seemingly found its groove. Unfortunately the remainder of the series was a succession of tough losses, culminating in a humiliating defeat in the decisive game. (Courtesy of the Boston Celtics.)

Forward Brian Scalabrine signed with the Celtics in the summer of 2005 as a free agent. The former University of Southern California star started his NBA career with the New Jersey Nets, where he served mostly as a backup before gradually assuming a starting role during the 2004–2005 season. (Courtesy of the Boston Celtics.)

The Celtics joined the ranks of most of their NBA competitors when they began signing high school players during the past decade. Included in their number is center Kendrick Perkins, who was originally chosen as the 27th pick in the 2003 NBA draft by the Memphis Grizzlies before being traded to the Celtics. The Celtics expect that Perkins, under the tutelage of Doc Rivers, will develop into a first-rank center. To date, the former Parade All-American has shown great promise. (Courtesy of the Boston Celtics.)

Boston fans, along with most basketball experts, were surprised when high school All-American Gerald Greene of Houston's Gulf Shores Academy became available for the Celtics to choose with the 18th overall pick of the 2005 NBA draft. The six-foot-eight-inch forward is considered one of best young players in basketball and a potential star in the making for the Celtics. (Courtesy of the Boston Celtics.)

In his first season as the Celtics head coach (2004–2005), Doc Rivers led Boston to its first Atlantic Division title since the 1991–1992 season. Prior to coaching the Celtics, Rivers enjoyed a 13-year career in the NBA, where he played for the Hawks, Clippers, Knicks, and Spurs. Following the end of his playing career, Rivers served as head coach of the Orlando Magic for five seasons, during which time he won the Red Auerbach Trophy as NBA Coach of the Year for the 1999–2000 season. (Courtesy of the Boston Globe.)

Waterbury, Connecticut, native Ryan Gomes was one of the steals of the 2005 NBA draft, being selected by the Celtics with the 50th overall pick in the second round. During the second half of his rookie season, the six-foot-seven-inch forward blossomed as he not only found his scoring touch but was rewarded with significant playing time. In his college career at Providence, Gomes departed as the Friars all-time leading scorer with 2,138 points. (Courtesy of the Boston Celtics.)

Before Wally Szczerbiak came to the Celtics in a trade in the middle of the 2005–2006 season, he had exhibited his great talent and shooting with the Minnesota Timberwolves. While a senior at Miami (Ohio) University, Szczerbiak finished his college career with the Mid-American Conference Player of the Year honors and left holding Miami's record for three-point field-goal percentage, with .431. His playing abilities continued to flourish in the NBA, earning him a place on the 1999–2000 Schick All-Rookie Team, which led to his role as a regular starter for Minnesota. (Courtesy of Sports Action Images.)

The intimate confines of the Boston Garden was the site for over 2,000 Celtics home games played in the first half century of the team's existence. It was here that forward Tony Lavelli played his accordion at halftime, Bob Cousy wept as he bade Boston farewell, Havlicek stole the ball, and Red Auerbach lit 9 of his 16 victory cigars in celebration of Celtics world championships. The Boston Garden was the city's theater of dreams. (Courtesy of the Sports Museum.)

# CHAMPIONS OF THE WORLD

The 1956–1957 world champions, from left to right, included the following: (first row) Lou Tsioropoulos, Andy Philip, Frank Ramsey, Red Auerbach, Bob Cousy, Bill Sharman, and Jim Loscutoff; (second row) Walter Brown, Dick Hemric, Jack Nichols, Bill Russell, Arnie Risen, Tommy Heinsohn, Harvey Cohn, and Lou Pieri. (Courtesy of the Boston Celtics.)

Regular Season: 44-28 (.611), +6, First Place

1957 Division Finals (3-0)
March 21 Syracuse (90) at Boston (108)
March 23 Boston (120) at Syracuse (105)
March 24 Syracuse (80) at Boston (83)

1957 Championship Finals (4-3)
March 30 St. Louis (125) at Boston (123), double overtime
March 31 St. Louis (99) at Boston (119)
April 6 Boston (98) at St. Louis (100)
April 7 Boston (123) at St. Louis (118)
April 9 St. Louis (109) at Boston (124)

April 11 Boston (94) at St. Louis (96)
April 13 St. Louis (123) at Boston (125), double overtime

The 1958–1959 world champions, from left to right, included the following: (first row) Lou Pieri (inset), Gene Conley, Bob Cousy, Red Auerbach, Walter Brown, Bill Sharman, and Bill Russell; (second row) Buddy LeRoux, K. C. Jones, Lou Tsioropoulos, Tom Heinsohn, Ben Swain, Jim Loscutoff, Sam Jones, and Frank Ramsey. (Courtesy of the Boston Celtics.)

Regular Season: 52-20 (.722), +12, First Place

1959 Division Finals (4-3)
March 18 Syracuse (109) at Boston (131)
March 21 Boston (118) at Syracuse (120)

March 22 Syracuse (111) at Boston (133)
March 25 Boston (107) at Syracuse (119)
March 28 Syracuse (108) at Boston (129)
March 29 Boston (121) at Syracuse (133)
April 1 Syracuse (125) at Boston (130)

1959 Championship Finals (4-0)
April 4 Minneapolis (115) at Boston (118)
April 5 Minneapolis (108) at Boston (128)
April 7 Boston (123) at Minneapolis (110)
April 9 Boston (118) at Minneapolis (113)

The 1959–1960 world champions, from left to right, included the following: (first row) Frank Ramsey, Bob Cousy, Red Auerbach, Walter Brown, Lou Pieri, K. C. Jones, and Bill Sharman; (second row) Gene Guarilia, Tom Heinsohn, John Richter, Bill Russell, Gene Conley, Jim Loscutoff, Sam Jones, and Buddy LeRoux. (Courtesy of the Boston Celtics.)

Regular Season: 59-16 (.787), +10, First Place

1960 Division Finals (4-2)
March 16 Philadelphia (105) at Boston (111)
March 18 Boston (110) at Philadelphia (115)
March 19 Philadelphia (90) at Boston (120)

March 20 Boston (112) at Philadelphia (104)
March 22 Philadelphia (128) at Boston (107)
March 24 Boston (119) at Philadelphia (117)

1960 Championship Finals (4-3)
March 27 St. Louis (122) at Boston (140)

March 29 St. Louis (113) at Boston (103)
April 2 Boston (102) at St. Louis (86)
April 3 Boston (96) at St. Louis (106)
April 5 St. Louis (102) at Boston (127)
April 7 Boston (102) at St. Louis (105)
April 9 St. Louis (103) at Boston (122)

The 1960–1961 world champions, from left to right, included the following: (first row) Lou Pieri (inset), K. C. Jones, Bob Cousy, Red Auerbach, Walter Brown, Bill Sharman, and Frank Ramsey; (second row) Buddy LeRoux, Tom Sanders, Tom Heinsohn, Gene Conley, Bill Russell, Gene Guarilia, Jim Loscutoff, and Sam Jones. (Courtesy of the Boston Celtics.)

Regular Season: 57-22 (.722), +11, First Place

1961 Division Finals (4-1)
March 19 Syracuse (115) at Boston (128)
March 21 Boston (98) at Syracuse (115)
March 23 Syracuse (110) at Boston (133)

March 25 Boston (120) at Syracuse (107)
March 26 Syracuse (101) at Boston (123)

1961 Championship Finals (4-1)
April 2 St. Louis (95) at Boston (129)
April 5 St. Louis (108) at Boston (116)

April 8 Boston (120) at St. Louis (124)
April 9 Boston (119) at St. Louis (104)
April 11 St. Louis (112) at Boston (121)

The 1961–1962 world champions, from left to right, included the following: (first row) K. C. Jones, Gary Philips, Walter Brown, Red Auerbach, Lou Pieri, Bob Cousy, and Sam Jones; (second row) Frank Ramsey, Tom Sanders, Tom Heinsohn, Bill Russell, Gene Guarilia, Jim Loscutoff, Carl Braun, and Buddy LeRoux. (Courtesy of the Boston Celtics.)

Regular Season: 60-20 (.750) +11, First Place

1962 Division Finals (4-3)
March 24 Philadelphia (89) at Boston (117)
March 27 Boston (106) at Philadelphia (113)
March 28 Philadelphia (114) at Boston (129)
March 31 Boston (106) at Philadelphia (110)

April 1 Philadelphia (104) at Boston (119)
April 3 Boston (99) at Philadelphia (109)
April 5 Philadelphia (107) at Boston (109)

1962 Championship Finals (4-3)
April 7 Los Angeles (108) at Boston (122)
April 8 Los Angeles (129) at Boston (122)

April 10 Boston (115) at Los Angeles (117)
April 11 Boston (115) at Los Angeles (103)
April 14 Los Angeles (126) at Boston (121)
April 16 Boston (119) at Los Angeles (105)
April 18 Los Angeles (107) at Boston (110), overtime

The 1962–1963 world champions, from left to right, included the following: (first row) K. C. Jones, Bill Russell, Walter Brown, Red Auerbach, Lou Pieri, Bob Cousy, and Sam Jones; (second row) Frank Ramsey, Gene Guarilia, Tom Sanders, Tom Heinsohn, Clyde Lovellette, John Havlicek, Jim Loscutoff, Dan Swartz, and Buddy LeRoux. (Courtesy of the Boston Celtics.)

Regular Season: 58-22 (.725), +10, First Place

1963 Division Finals (4-3)
March 28 Cincinnati (135) at Boston (132)
March 29 Boston (125) at Cincinnati (102)
March 31 Cincinnati (121) at Boston (116)
April 3 Boston (128) at Cincinnati (110)

April 6 Cincinnati (110) at Boston (125)
April 7 Boston (99) at Cincinnati (109)
April 10 Cincinnati (131) at Boston (142)

1963 Championship Finals (4-2)
April 14 Los Angeles (114) at Boston (117)
April 16 Los Angeles (106) at Boston (113)

April 17 Boston (99) at Los Angeles (119)
April 19 Boston (108) at Los Angeles (105)
April 21 Los Angeles (126) at Boston (119)
April 24 Boston (112) at Los Angeles (109)

The 1963–1964 world champions, from left to right, included the following: (first row) Sam Jones, Frank Ramsey, K. C. Jones, Red Auerbach, Walter Brown, Bill Russell, and John Havlicek; (second row) John McCarthy, Tom Sanders, Tom Heinsohn, Clyde Lovellette, Willie Naulls, Jim Loscutoff, Larry Siegfried, and Buddy LeRoux. (Courtesy of the Boston Celtics.)

Regular Season: 59-21 (.738), +4, First Place

1964 Division Finals (4-1)
March 31 Cincinnati (87) at Boston (103)
April 2 Cincinnati (90) at Boston (101)
April 5 Boston (102) at Cincinnati (92)

April 7 Boston (93) at Cincinnati (102)
April 9 Cincinnati (95) at Boston (109)

1964 Championship Finals (4-1)
April 18 San Francisco (96) at Boston (108)
April 20 San Francisco (101) at Boston (124)

April 22 Boston (91) at San Francisco (115)
April 24 Boston (98) at San Francisco (95)
April 26 San Francisco (99) at Boston (105)

The 1964–1965 world champions, from left to right, included the following: (first row) K. C. Jones, Tom Heinsohn, Lou Pieri, Red Auerbach, Bill Russell, and Sam Jones; (second row) Ron Bonham, Larry Siegfried, Willie Naulls, Mel Counts, John Thompson, Tom Sanders, John Havlicek, and Buddy LeRoux. (Courtesy of the Boston Celtics.)

Regular Season: 62-18 (.755), +14, First Place

1965 Division Finals (4-3)
April 4 Philadelphia (98) at Boston (108)
April 6 Boston (103) at Philadelphia (109)
April 8 Philadelphia (94) at Boston (112)
April 9 Boston (131) at Philadelphia (134)

April 11 Philadelphia (108) at Boston (114)
April 13 Boston (106) at Philadelphia (112)
April 15 Philadelphia (109) at Boston (110)

1965 Championship Finals (4-1)
April 18 Los Angeles (110) at Boston (142)
April 19 Los Angeles (123) at Boston (129)

April 21 Boston (105) at Los Angeles (126)
April 23 Boston (112) at Los Angeles (99)
April 25 Los Angeles (96) at Boston (129)

The 1965–1966 world champions, from left to right, included the following: (first row) John Havlicek, K. C. Jones, Marvin Kratter, Red Auerbach, Jack Waldron, and Bill Russell; (second row) Ron Bonham, Don Nelson, Tom Sanders, Mel Counts, John Thompson, Woody Sauldsberry, Willie Naulls, Sam Jones, Larry Siegfried, and Buddy LeRoux. (Courtesy of the Boston Celtics.)

Regular Season: 54-26 (.675), -1, Second Place

1966 Division Semifinals (3-2)
March 23 Cincinnati (107) at Boston (103)
March 26 Boston (132) at Cincinnati (125)
March 27 Cincinnati (113) at Boston (107)
March 30 Boston (120) at Cincinnati (103)
April 1 Cincinnati (103) at Boston (112)

1966 Division Finals (4-1)
April 3 Boston (115) at Philadelphia (96)

April 6 Philadelphia (93) at Boston (114)
April 7 Boston (105) at Philadelphia (111)
April 10 Philadelphia (108) at Boston (114), overtime
April 12 Boston (120) at Philadelphia (112)

1966 Championship Finals (4-3)
April 17 Los Angeles (133) at Boston (129), overtime
April 19 Los Angeles (109) at Boston (129)
April 20 Boston (120) at Los Angeles (106)
April 22 Boston (122) at Los Angeles (117)
April 24 Los Angeles (121) at Boston (117)

April 26 Boston (115) at Los Angeles (123)
April 28 Los Angeles (93) at Boston (95)

The 1967–1968 world champions, from left to right, included the following: (first row) Sam Jones, Larry Siegfried, Red Auerbach, Marvin Kratter, Clarence Adams, Bill Russell, and John Havlicek; (second row) Joe DeLauri, Rick Weitzman, Tom Thacker, Tom Sanders, Bailey Howell, Wayne Embry, Don Nelson, John Jones, and Mal Graham. (Courtesy of the Boston Celtics.)

Regular Season: 54-28 (.659), -8, Second Place

1968 Division Semifinals (4-2)
March 24 Detroit (116) at Boston (123)
March 25 Boston (116) at Detroit (126)
March 27 Detroit (109) at Boston (98)
March 28 Boston (135) at Detroit (110)
March 31 Detroit (96) at Boston (110)
April 1 Boston (111) at Detroit (103)

1968 Division Finals (4-3)
April 5 Boston (127) at Philadelphia (118)
April 10 Philadelphia (115) at Boston (106)
April 11 Boston (114) at Philadelphia (122)
April 14 Philadelphia (110) at Boston (105)
April 15 Boston (122) at Philadelphia (104)
April 17 Philadelphia (106) at Boston (114)
April 19 Boston (100) at Philadelphia (96)

1968 Championship Finals (4-2)
April 21 Los Angeles (101) at Boston (107)
April 24 Los Angeles (123) at Boston (113)
April 26 Boston (127) at Los Angeles (119)
April 28 Boston (105) at Los Angeles (119)
April 30 Los Angeles (117) at Boston (120), overtime
May 2 Boston (124) at Los Angeles (109)

The 1968–1969 world champions, from left to right, included the following: (first row) Don Nelson, Sam Jones, Bill Russell, Jack Waldron, Red Auerbach, John Havlicek, Dr. Thomas Silva, and Larry Siegfried; (second row) Joe DeLauri, Emmette Bryant, Don Chaney, Tom Sanders, Rich Johnson, Jim Barnes, Bailey Howell, and Mal Graham. (Courtesy of the Boston Celtics.)

Regular Season: 48-34 (.585), -9, Fourth Place

1969 Division Semifinals (4-1)
March 26 Boston (114) at Philadelphia (100)
March 28 Philadelphia (103) at Boston (134)
March 30 Boston (125) at Philadelphia (118)
April 1 Philadelphia (119) at Boston (116)
April 4 Boston (93) at Philadelphia (90)

1969 Division Finals (4-2)
April 6 Boston (108) at New York (100)
April 9 New York (97) at Boston (112)
April 10 Boston (91) at New York (101)
April 13 New York (96) at Boston (97)
April 14 Boston (104) at New York (112)
April 18 New York (105) at Boston (106)

1969 Championship Finals (4-3)
April 23 Boston (118) at Los Angeles (120)
April 25 Boston (112) at Los Angeles (118)
April 27 Los Angeles (105) at Boston (111)
April 29 Los Angeles (88) at Boston (89)
May 1 Boston (104) at Los Angeles (117)
May 3 Los Angeles (90) at Boston (99)
May 5 Boston (108) at Los Angeles (106)

The 1973–1974 world champions, from left to right, included the following: (first row) JoJo White, Don Chaney, John Havlicek, Red Auerbach, Robert Schmertz, Tom Heinsohn, Dave Cowens, Paul Silas, and John Killilea; (second row) Mark Volk, Dr. Sam Kane, Paul Westphal, Phil Hankinson, Steve Downing, Don Nelson, Hank Finkel, Steve Kuberski, Art Williams, Dr. Thomas Silva, and Frank Challant. (Courtesy of the Boston Celtics.)

Regular Season 56-26 (.683), +7, First Place

1974 Conference Semifinals (4-2)
March 30 Buffalo (97) at Boston (107)
April 2 Boston (105) at Buffalo (115)
April 3 Buffalo (107) at Boston (120)
April 6 Boston (102) at Buffalo (104)
April 9 Buffalo (97) at Boston (100)
April 12 Boston (106) at Buffalo (104)

1974 Conference Finals (4-1)
April 14 New York (88) at Boston (113)
April 16 Boston (111) at New York (99)
April 19 New York (103) at Boston (100)
April 21 Boston (98) at New York (91)
April 24 New York (94) at Boston (105)

1974 Championship Finals (4-3)
April 28 Boston (98) at Milwaukee (83)
April 30 Boston (96) at Milwaukee (105), overtime

May 3 Milwaukee (83) at Boston (95)
May 5 Milwaukee (97) at Boston (89)
May 7 Boston (96) at Milwaukee (87)
May 10 Milwaukee (102) at Boston (101), double overtime
May 12 Boston (102) at Milwaukee (87)

The 1975–1976 world champions, from left to right, included the following: (first row) Charlie Scott, Paul Silas, Dave Cowens, Irving Levin, Tom Heinsohn, Red Auerbach, John Havlicek, JoJo White, and Don Nelson; (second row) Dr. Thomas Silva, Mark Volk, Kevin Stacom, Glenn McDonald, Tom Boswell, Jim Ard, Steve Kuberski, Jerome Anderson, Frank Challant, and Dr. Sam Kane. (Courtesy of the Boston Celtics.)

Regular Season 54-28 (.659), +8, First Place

1976 Conference Semifinals (4-2)
April 21 Buffalo (98) at Boston (107)
April 23 Buffalo (96) at Boston (101)
April 25 Boston (93) at Buffalo (98)
April 28 Boston (122) at Buffalo (124)
April 30 Buffalo (88) at Boston (99)
May 2 Boston (104) at Buffalo (100)

1976 Conference Finals (4-2)
May 6 Cleveland (99) at Boston (111)
May 9 Cleveland (89) at Boston (94)
May 11 Boston (78) at Cleveland (83)
May 14 Boston (87) at Cleveland (106)
May 16 Cleveland (94) at Boston (99)
May 18 Boston (94) at Cleveland (87)

1976 Championship Finals (4-2)
May 23 Phoenix (87) at Boston (98)
May 27 Phoenix (90) at Boston (105)
May 30 Boston (98) at Phoenix (105)
June 2 Boston (107) at Phoenix (109)
June 4 Phoenix (126) at Boston (128), triple overtime
June 6 Boston (87) at Phoenix (80)

The 1980–1981 world champions, from left to right, included the following: (first row) Chris Ford, Cedric Maxwell, Red Auerbach, Bill Fitch, Harry Mangurian, Larry Bird, and Nate Archibald; (second row) K. C. Jones, Wayne Kreklow, M. L. Carr, Rick Robey, Robert Parish, Kevin McHale, Eric Fernsten, Gerald Henderson, Jim Rodgers, and Ray Melchiorre. (Courtesy of the Boston Celtics.)

Regular Season 62-20 (.756), Tied for First Place

1981 Conference Semifinals (4-0)
April 5 Chicago (109) at Boston (121)
April 7 Chicago (97) at Boston (106)
April 10 Boston (113) at Chicago (107)
April 12 Boston (109) at Chicago (103)

1981 Conference Finals (4-3)
April 21 Philadelphia (105) at Boston (104)
April 22 Philadelphia (99) at Boston (118)
April 24 Boston (100) at Philadelphia (110)
April 26 Boston (105) at Philadelphia (107)
April 29 Philadelphia (109) at Boston (111)
May 1 Boston (100) at Philadelphia (98)
May 3 Philadelphia (90) at Boston (91)

1981 Championship Finals (4-2)
May 5 Houston (95) at Boston (98)
May 7 Houston (92) at Boston (90)
May 9 Boston (94) at Houston (71)
May 10 Boston (86) at Houston (91)
May 12 Houston (80) at Boston (109)
May 14 Boston (102) at Houston (91)

The 1983–1984 world champions, from left to right, included the following: (first row) Quinn Buckner, Cedric Maxwell, Paul R. Dupee, Don F. Gaston, Red Auerbach, K. C. Jones, Alan Cohen, Larry Bird, and M. L. Carr; (second row) Dr. Thomas Silva, Jim Rodgers, Gerald Henderson, Scott Wedman, Greg Kite, Robert Parish, Kevin McHale, Dennis Johnson, Danny Ainge, Carlos Clark, Chris Ford, and Ray Melchiorre. (Courtesy of the Boston Celtics.)

Regular Season 62-20 (.756), +10, First Place

1984 Eastern Conference First Round (3-1)
April 17 Washington (83) at Boston (91)
April 19 Washington (85) at Boston (88)
April 21 Boston (108) at Washington (111), overtime
April 24 Boston (99) at Washington (96)

1984 Eastern Conference Semifinals (4-3)
April 29 New York (92) at Boston (110)
May 2 New York (102) at Boston (116)
May 4 Boston (92) at New York (100)
May 6 Boston (113) at New York (118)
May 9 New York (99) at Boston (121)
May 11 Boston (104) at New York (106)
May 13 New York (104) at Boston (121)

1984 Eastern Conference Championship (4-1)
May 15 Milwaukee (96) at Boston (119)
May 17 Milwaukee (110) at Boston (125)
May 19 Boston (109) at Milwaukee (100)
May 21 Boston (113) at Milwaukee (122)
May 23 Milwaukee (108) at Boston (115)

1984 NBA World Championship Series (4-3)
May 27 Los Angeles (115) at Boston (109)
May 31 Los Angeles (121) at Boston (124), overtime
June 3 Boston (104) at Los Angeles (137)
June 6 Boston (129) at Los Angeles (125), overtime
June 8 Los Angeles (103) at Boston (121)
June 10 Boston (108) at Los Angeles (119)
June 12 Los Angeles (102) at Boston (111)

The 1985–1986 world champions, from left to right, included the following: (first row) Danny Ainge, Scott Wedman, Alan Cohen, Jan Volk, Red Auerbach, K. C. Jones, Don F. Gaston, Larry Bird, and Dennis Johnson; (second row) Wayne LeBeaux, Dr. Thomas Silva, Jim Rodgers, Sam Vincent, Rick Carlisle, Greg Kite, Robert Parish, Bill Walton, Kevin McHale, David Thirdkill, Jerry Sichting, Chris Ford, and Ray Melchiorre. (Courtesy of the Boston Celtics.)

Regular Season 67-15 (.817), +13, First Place

1986 Eastern Conference First Round (3-0)
April 17 Chicago (104) at Boston (123)
April 20 Chicago (131) at Boston (135), double overtime
April 22 Boston (122) at Chicago (104)

1986 Eastern Conference Semifinals (4-1)
April 27 Atlanta (91) at Boston (103)
April 29 Atlanta (108) at Boston (119)

May 2 Boston (111) at Atlanta (107)
May 4 Boston (94) at Atlanta (106)
May 6 Atlanta (99) at Boston (132)

1986 Eastern Conference Finals (4-0)
May 13 Milwaukee (96) at Boston (128)
May 15 Milwaukee (111) at Boston (122)
May 17 Boston (111) at Milwaukee (107)
May 18 Boston (111) at Milwaukee (98)

1986 NBA Finals (4-2)
May 26 Houston (100) at Boston (112)
May 29 Houston (95) at Boston (117)
June 1 Boston (104) at Houston (106)
June 3 Boston (106) at Houston (103)
June 5 Boston (96) at Houston (111)
June 8 Houston (97) at Boston (114)

NBA commissioner Larry O'Brien presents the NBA
championship trophy that bears his name to Celtics owner
Harry Mangurian (center) and Celtics president Red
Auerbach (right). (Courtesy of the Boston Herald.)

# DISCOVER THOUSANDS OF LOCAL HISTORY BOOKS FEATURING MILLIONS OF VINTAGE IMAGES

Arcadia Publishing, the leading local history publisher in the United States, is committed to making history accessible and meaningful through publishing books that celebrate and preserve the heritage of America's people and places.

Find more books like this at
**www.arcadiapublishing.com**

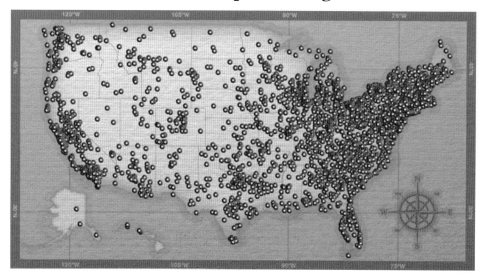

Search for your hometown history, your old stomping grounds, and even your favorite sports team.

Consistent with our mission to preserve history on a local level, this book was printed in South Carolina on American-made paper and manufactured entirely in the United States. Products carrying the accredited Forest Stewardship Council (FSC) label are printed on 100 percent FSC-certified paper.

MADE IN THE USA